Tired, Hungry, Standing in One Spot for Twelve Hours: **ESSENTIAL COP ESSAYS**

Sarah Cortez

Texas Review Press
Huntsville, Texas

FIRST EDITION
Requests for permission to acknowledge material from this work should be sent to:

Permissions
Texas Review Press
English Department
Sam Houston State University
Huntsville, TX 77341-2146

Cover Design by Nancy Parsons

Library of Congress Cataloging-in-Publication Data

Names: Cortez, Sarah, author.
Title: Tired, hungry, and standing in one spot for twelve hours : essential cop essays / Sarah Cortez.
Description: First edition. | Huntsville, Texas : Texas Review Press, [2018] Identifiers: LCCN 2017055382 (print) | LCCN 2017056331 (ebook) | ISBN 9781680031447 (ebook) | ISBN 9781680031430 | ISBN 9781680031430¨(pbk.)
Subjects: LCSH: Cortez, Sarah. | Policewomen--Texas--Houston--Biography. | Police--Texas--Houston--Biography. | Hispanic American women authors--21st century--Biography. | Authors, American--21st century--Biography. | LCGFT: Autobiography.
Classification: LCC PS3553.O7227 (ebook) | LCC PS3553.O7227 Z46 2018 (print) | DDC 818/.603 [B] --dc23

LC record available at https://lccn.loc.gov/2017055382

For the almost one million men and women in America who, each day and night, strap on a gun, place a badge over a heart or on a waistband, and go out to police the mean streets.

Tired, Hungry, Standing in One Spot for Twelve Hours: **ESSENTIAL COP ESSAYS**

Table of Contents

Section One

Introduction 1

Chapter One 5

Chapter Two 9

Chapter Three, Academy Floors 13

Chapter Four 22

Section Two

My Work Week 29

My Gender 36

Our Stories 44

Knife-Girl 49

One Woman 53

Kitchen Hungers 60

Acquainted with Death 66

Supervisors 77

Here Are My Lists 86

After Many Years 91

Glossary and Abbreviations 97

Preface

There are many friends who have supported this work in crucial ways. First, I would like to thank my fellow police officers and supervisors: Assistant Chief Kenneth Key, Lt. Darrell Butler, Sgt. Jeff Lee, Deputies Gary Chambers, Donna Douglass, Perri Marsh, (ret.) David McBroom, Sean Richardson, and (deceased) Sgt. Bob Johnson and (deceased) Lt. Lanny Shepard.

Secondly, I would like to thank my fellow writers who have assisted me in innumerable ways through critique and incredible intangible support: Carolyn Dahl, Phyllis Ferguson, Lt. Betsy Randolph (Oklahoma Highway Patrol), T.K. Thorne, and Germaine Welch, Ph.D.

One of these essays entitled "My Gender" has been previously published in another form in *Her Texas: Story, Image, Poem & Song*, edited by Donna Walker-Nixon, Cassy Burleson, Rachel Crawford, Ashley Palmer (2015).

The essay "Acquainted with Death" was designated a semi-finalist in the 2018 Tucson Festival of Books Literary Awards in Nonfiction.

Section One

Introduction

I hear a patrol car's throaty V-8 approach from behind, its chassis squeaking slightly.

Turning, I see one of the tall, solid police officers driving a blue-and-white unevenly over potholes behind HPD's Central Police Station.

He pulls up next to me as the radials crunch through asphalt and throw small rocks to the side. The orangish glow of artificial lighting under low, dense clouds colors us both faintly unreal. His face and hands become visible within the car's dark interior. They are abnormally pale from years working deep nights—the shadows and gloom have long since replaced his sunlight. Not for the first time am I aware that my tidy, safe life is totally uninformed by the repetitive reality of high-speed chases, undercover special assignments, fist fights, and volatile domestics.

I've met him before; he's a nice guy—the best friend of another officer I know well. They both have worked in policing their entire lives. As far as I know, there isn't a single person, place, or thing inside their universe that's more important than this job.

He flashes a smile that fades immediately; his blue eyes don't soften. The steel inside of them doesn't want to melt, or can't. My thoughts fly to what he's seen on the job. No wonder he seems unshakeable—a predictable gift from his years of patrol experience. Whether you call it tactical awareness or intuition or street smarts or something else, he has it. He's earned it the only way it can be earned—the hard way. Everyone senses it in the way he walks and talks, looks at people, enters a room. It probably even has changed the way he sleeps, and how and what he eats—how could it not? The understanding of how to survive the streets is so deeply embedded in his muscles, mind, and memory that he doesn't have to think about it. It simply exists inside of him like an infinity clock that never needs rewinding. Survival has become his auto-pilot; integrity for serving this one purpose has honed his reflexes.

What will happen if I reveal to him the secret inside of me? This internal blaze that is threatening to conflagrate my corporate career, my marriage, my entire existence. This deeper-than-deep dream I have that is too strong to be changed by sex or love or money—believe me, I've tried. Can I tell him?

The huge rush of hopeful words in my heart becomes an abbreviated, terse sentence: "Chuck, I want to be a cop."

His light blue eyes go quieter. The entire, living mechanism of his body stills. He doesn't appear to breathe. Nothing falters in a gaze that has become apprising. I focus on each freckle across his huge knuckles on the patrol car's steering wheel. His short, clipped nails; his thick fingers with no rings.

I eagerly recite the extensive list of assets I possess for what I hope will become my new life in law enforcement: excellent physical shape, attention to detail, conversational Spanish—sort of. He stares. The seriousness of his demeanor breaks me off mid-sentence.

"Sarah," he says, exhaling a long, tired breath, "Can you dust someone?"

It takes me a few seconds too long to figure out what he's

saying. He's asking me if I can kill someone. His posture is now pointer-dog alert against the worn blue seat cover.

"Yes, Chuck. I can do that."

"You better be sure. Your life or someone else's may depend on it."

He rubs the faint beads of sweat from his upper lip and cranks up the A/C against Houston's humidity. Here, behind the police station the eerie glow of Houston's skyscrapers feels viscous, faintly poisoned.

He's shaven closely—like all the cops I've met. The little curls on the back of his head are damp—probably from the shower in the station's decrepit gym. The faint pine-fresh smell of soap drifts out the car's window.

I don't know what else to say.

He glances at his watch. "If you know yourself good enough to know the answer, you'll be fine."

A little glimmer of life returns to his eyes. "I gotta go. See you later." He slaps the visor up into precarious alignment. "Let me know how I can help."

His blue-and-white, spewing gravel, roars off across the lot. Its power curls around my heart and tugs. One day I'll drive my own heavy-bodied, wide-ass patrol car. One day I'll open its car door, place my scuffed boots on the ground, and walk the lawman's walk into danger.

Tonight, in an untended, deserted parking lot, this man I respect has already helped me. He asked the right question at the right time. A question spawned from his years of living the job from the inside out.

What he has really asked, of course, is whether I have thought about the incredible responsibility of wearing a gun and enforcing the law. He really asked if I'll get hysterical, if I'll have a case of nerves or be paralyzed when decisive action is required. What he really asked is can I be solid to my core when every ounce of shit hits the fan. *Can I do what is necessary?*

He didn't ask if I was scared to die or get injured. He didn't ask if I could roll on the roadside with a drunk or would I mind having my ass kicked by the same. He asked the purest question of duty there is for police: can you kill to save your life or someone else's? This ultimate question demands probing the depths of self. Finding the answer is as hard as going so deep to find it.

I trust his question, and I trust my answer. I know what I will do and what I won't do. This knowledge will protect me. And if it doesn't? Well, I'll deal with that later.

For now, I know I've plunged inward as far as I can figure to go to locate the most profound substrate of meaning and value I can find inside myself. I've spent months searching for what was my own version of unshakable and profound. And to that same internal place I took the all-important, ethical questions I had to know the answers to *before* I considered this change which is so much more than a career change. For me, and so many others, going into law enforcement is a calling. A vocational pull stronger than gravity into a gritty world where we hope to do the most good with what God has given us physically, emotionally, and mentally. It's not a job for everyone, nor should it be.

My course is set. I know what I need to know about myself. Everything else I can learn.

I will become a police officer.

Chapter One

In the two years surrounding my decision to become a police officer, I met numerous police officers and their supervisors. Crusty, gravel-voiced veterans whose faces would break into quick, thin-lipped smiles below mirrored aviators. On a whole, they welcomed me. To their credit, they didn't pretend that policing was easy or glamorous or necessarily heroic. They didn't even fake solutions to every human tragedy. By observing them and listening, I saw how much could be accomplished by a stoic commitment to handling whatever a call-for-service threw at them.

I drank in knowledge of the hard-edged, metallic world they inhabited. Compared to my overly and overtly intellectual career, the blue-collar world was common-sense, although not necessarily predicable and certainly not simple.

For instance, one sergeant I met for a short lunch while he was on day-shift patrol refused to walk inside my house when he came over. I asked why. He replied that he'd just come from a call-for-service involving an elderly W/F (white female) who kept multiple dogs and cats inside her home and he'd just walked through all kinds of piss and shit on her carpet. He sheepishly looked down at his size-thirteen boots and said, "I know where these have been.

You don't want them on your floor." He was right—I didn't want all that across my rugs or polished hardwood. Yet, I liked the unpredictability of what these men saw and did.

My childhood had contained one gigantic red-headed Irish police officer of my dad's generation who came to the house for coffee and dessert with his lovely wife and daughter. We all respected him, but that was a generation where, in my parents' household, you respected everyone. Mostly, he and my dad told good-natured hunting and fishing stories set on the beautiful Gulf shores and coastal lakes near Houston. I remember an abundance of red-lipstick smiles over china coffee cups at the mahogany dinner table, wreathes of laughter on the dark-headed wives.

But all those young experiences with my dad's Irish friend from WWII was before a crime wave overtook the neighborhood where I lived in the 1980s, which coincided with a push in the Houston Police Department to reach out and strategize proactive crime-fighting in partnership with civic groups.

There we were: two groups trying to understand each other—the police officers in powder-blue shirts, shiny black patent leather belts and polished Ropers, and us volunteers from a neighborhood association. Our goal was the same: increased safety for ourselves and our historic bungalows on tree-lined avenues now backed by prostitute-and-drug-filled alleyways.

We sat crammed into wooden desks in a narrow classroom in the Houston Central Police Station. These tall, muscular officers would sit sideways at a thirty-degree angle to fit their gun belts and guns into the old-fashioned desks designed for trimmer, unarmed occupants. Even so, they listened to us and listened well as we recited the long laundry list of spill-over crimes from the illegal sex and drug activity. We listened to them as well, learning bit by bit what took place on our streets and in our yards while we slept and were at work. Fascinating peeks at a world far more interesting, far more challenging than the smooth domesticity of my life.

I was secretly enthralled with decoding the alluring visual language of policing—creased trousers, round-toed, black boots buffed to parade gloss, stacked brass over a right pocket. The metallic imperative of items attached to the gun belt: handcuffs, keys, a baton—all of which occasionally jingled or clanked giving each officer his own unique melody of small movements. The square silver buckle in front of the gun belt where almost all the officers inserted the patrol car's ignition key at a horizontal when they were out of the vehicle. The metal shop tag fluttering like a small, innocent flag across flat stomachs.

I learned how to tell rank by the silver (patrol officers and sergeants) or gold (LT's and above) glinting off the edges of name plates, bars, badges, or shields. Length of service time in the department was displayed in hash marks, like half a chevron, sewn on the forearms of long-sleeved shirts. All of this—a complex but discernible vocabulary of sharp angles and boxy letters—built on the essential need for quick perception of the formalized chain of command. A requisite intersection of behavior and respect.

I began to see the intimate relationship between the body and mind of the patrol officer and his uniform. The best I can explain it is that the uniform was something a man "lived up to" rather than "lived inside of." What the uniform stood for was always bigger than the person wearing it—selfless duty, impeccable integrity, loyal service. If you let it, the uniform could call you higher—up to the highest ideals of the profession.

These police officers I met were willing to do so much that regular people wouldn't do—disarm suicides-in-progress, deal with razor-wielding crazies, search abandoned buildings in the middle of the night, jump into bayous to save a drowning person. How could I not respond to this self-possessed coolness in the face of potential injury and death? How could I not respond to their unruffled examples of the right thing, done in the right way, for the right reasons.

I fell in love with policing, and I fell hard. Undeniably, part of it was that sharp para-military uniform representing the profession, the close ranks of those committed to the same goal. But a bigger and more crucial part was the crime-fighting itself. Ride-alongs with street cops gave me glimpses into a nightly world of drug deals, teens turning tricks, domestics, agg assaults, gang fights, and messy drunks. Just enough to whet my appetite and send my imagination spinning: What would it be like to inhabit society's underbelly every night? Could I be the strong, silent protector? How would I handle *that* call for service? What would I do when a scene went south?

Once my heart changed, I had to follow it—not that it was easy. The practicalities of getting in top shape, taking a radical pay cut, and applying to a police academy were simply the sacrifices required. The eventual payoff would be wearing the uniform and doing the job. All I wanted was the chance to become a cop. The chance to prove myself in an unfamiliar environment where the stakes would be high and the external rewards minimal. And the internal rewards?? This is where my heart didn't hesitate—it understood intangibles and it already cherished duty, loyalty, and courage. After all, all my uncles had served in WWII or Korea—the only one too young to join had lied about his age to enlist. The unspoken rewards of doing the job well would be enough for me, or so I hoped.

Chapter 2

Many hard months later I was a member of Class 99 in the police academy. We wore the cadet uniforms—long-sleeved gray shirts, clip-on black ties, black trousers, black web belts, and, of course, black Ropers. Regulation black sweat pants and T-shirts with a yellow emblem for PT (physical training). Our drill instructors made sure we mastered the mysteries of a perfect gig line for buttons-buckle-zipper (which I still find myself checking out when any man enters the room). We learned the intricacies of a hand shine for those black Ropers insured by parade-gloss shoe polish, soft-bristled toothbrushes, cigarette lighters, horse-hair brushes, and endless buffing. Even after graduation, I recall Friday-night dates with good-looking police officers when the first thing we did was polish my boots. I held up my black Ropers beside a tin of polish on the kitchen countertop already spread with newspapers when they came through the front door of the house. *Show me*, I said. *Show me how you get a shine on your boots.* Then we would sit cross-legged, and I'd learn their tricks. Each of them, grinning at first, then becoming intent and intense during the application of polish, and then in the close-eyed details of timing, brushing, and finishing.

We cadets helped each other by sharing clothes brushes for lint, tins of shoe polish, "throw-down" black ties with pre-fab Windsor knots backed by a clip so we couldn't be strangled, and endless pairs of boot socks. Our headaches needed handfuls of aspirin slurped down with the warmish water from the water fountains in long, linoleum hallways.

The more experienced cops who were faculty were eager to share war stories as well as practical pointers about gear.

For instance, Ropers look good and are comfortable footwear for patrol work, but if you're chasing a suspect on a rainy pea-gravel sidewalk, you'll skid and not be able to corner. Hello, Mr. Groin Pull, or worse.

Another for instance, from a senior female street sergeant: No need to wear a bra under a ballistic vest because the vest shapes your boobs into an angled ship's prow—as head-edged as a carved, eighteenth-century ship's figurehead, and at roughly the same angle. In the vest—if you're female—everyone wants to hump you. A total pain.

What we learned from thick books with small type was made urgent and jarring by the stories we heard—the calls gone wrong, the officers killed or injured. We watched videos of police officers getting gunned down, knifed, crushed by speeding vehicles. Everything we learned had a cautionary tale behind it—an officer or jailer hurt, disabled, or worse. We learned permanent brain injury can be caused by twenty seconds of pressure on the carotids. We learned and learned and learned, trying to stuff our brains with every detail of what had ever gone wrong for another police officer, investigator, or state trooper—from any state. The goal—survival. The game—deadly.

Each instructor brought his or her own technical specialty—Homicide, Sex Crimes, Juvie, TABC (Texas Alcoholic Beverage Commission)—but I saw in each one an internal accommodation to policing that was even more fascinating to me. Did every cadet see it as I did? I never inquired. But what I saw and sensed set galaxies spinning in my private universe. The precise ways in which the Homicide detective's eyes were dead, deadened, as if all the deaths he'd worked had killed something vital inside him too. The experienced female Patrol sergeant from a smaller city south of Houston. The humorous and matter-of-fact way her voice described having to arrest a W/F giving a blow job to a dog up on stage at one of the illegal clubs. The particular way the dog was grinning. The handsome eagerness of a tall, young TABC investigator to close bars that sold to minors. The DWIs he hoped to prevent; the lives he hoped to save. Later I heard this same guy killed himself by driving at a high rate of speed into a tree—right after he'd been diagnosed with cancer—just two or three years after my Academy. Rumor was, he wanted his recent bride to get the insurance money—so he had to make it look like a traffic accident.

These stories were used to harden us to the reality of what happens on the streets—these things that most law-abiding people don't realize occur. We were also led through the steps of thinking through each situation tactically: placement, manpower, body language, weapons, motive, suspects, resources.

Tactical problem: large, drunk crowd. Popular entertainment. Suspect on stage with large K-9. Six police officers. One exit. Dim lighting.

Tactical solution: wait until break in action. Have female officer escort female suspect to exit. Cuff and stuff out of crowd's visual. Get towel/blanket/robe for suspect. Leave K-9 at scene but get descriptors for report. Leave scene; car with suspect leaves first. Meet at station.

There was no let-up except through humor. Maybe this is the wellspring of the famous cop humor—this need to relieve the stress inside with something laughable. Even if that something isn't PC, isn't gender-neutral, isn't squeaky clean. Life isn't clean; most people out there aren't well-intentioned or, even, by most standards relatively sane. We learned that the only sanity we could reasonably be expected to maintain was our own—and humor helped a lot with this demanding chore. Plus, as my good friend and experienced police supervisor Jeff would later say, "Everyone does stupid shit when a scene goes hinky. You got to laugh at yourself. You'll work with these guys a long time."

Chapter Three

Academy Floors

Large, pale yellow tiles. Perfect buttery squares encased in white grout. This sixth-floor bathroom at the police academy must have been pretty—once upon a time. Even now, these floor tiles could've been a touch of brightness for us, the few female police cadets who hit them at a run each night, scattering like buckshot, each to a stall. But, no. Puddles of water from broken toilets gave even these bright colors an overwhelming stench. There wasn't enough time to sprint to a bathroom on another floor, so I would hold my breath, and try to keep my perfectly shined, black Ropers clear of the larger puddles, then try to get my starched, long-sleeved shirt tucked back into my trousers with all the creases aligned just so, then finally wash my hands. It was of no use. There was no getting through on just one breath, or without some of that foulness clinging to the leather soles of my new boots.

Then one night another female cadet said she hated the way the restroom smelled like menstrual blood all the time. Bingo! That was it. Urgently stale, a smell whose subterranean taint was as penetrating as pervasive. The reminder of warm blood on a pad too long. After that, I could not walk into the yellow-tiled room without somehow looking for the maroon stain of darkened blood across the misleading cheeriness.

Was it the institutional grayness of bathroom stalls and countertops that made the yellow depressing? Was it the lingering, bloodied odor or the fact that no one cared enough to fix the plumbing? Maybe it was our grinding schedule? Working all day, attending night-school four nights a week, and non-stop memorization of the law for half the night. Maybe it made all of us gray ourselves in every aspect of emotion and mood?

My body responded by losing any appetite for food, so I became thinner but stronger. I worked out more, finding solace in repetitions of bicep curls, sit-ups, and squats. Most of the other female cadets filled out into more curvaceous versions of themselves, groaning as they pulled up sweat pants each night and cursing the cheap nachos covered in sour cream and congealed yellow cheese they ate before classes. *Cortez, you look good*, they'd say before pulling their sweat pants higher. *Damn, I wish I looked as good as you.* I couldn't take the compliments seriously. It was simply that my stomach wouldn't tolerate food before class. There were plenty of reasons—I was broke and separated from my husband. Sometimes, I slept in the spare bedroom at my parents' home refusing to think about the troubling implications of a grown, married woman sleeping in the same bed as when she had been an innocent teenager. At this point in my life, a safe road home didn't exist for me—not job-wise, not marriage-wise. I had to make this work for me—a new career, even if it was as improbable as it was dangerous. Too much was riding on my shoulders to be able to eat. I could barely choke down half a peanut-butter-and-jelly sandwich for lunch each day.

* * *

The asphalt is rough and uneven, poorly poured and disintegrating under the pooling rainwater here beneath the grimy overpass. This knobby black surface is where we gather for PT most class nights, all of us in short-sleeved, black T-shirts with yellow emblems, black sweatpants, and jogging shoes we're responsible for changing out in the bathrooms at 2100 hours, so we can conclude the night's classes on athletic exhilaration.

Every night we run in formation, two by two, singing to our DI's (drill instructor) chant—just like in the heroic movies about boot camp. I've been a jogger for years, so the easy cadence is pleasurable—a three-mile reward after another day of a tedious job and too little sleep. Sometimes, on these runs through Houston's downtown concrete corridors, our class captain, Goffney, barks like a big poodle—his specialty. We respond in our own individual canine growls, barks, and whimpers, so that the deserted streets echo with a slightly manic but joyously insistent rendition of a dog pack. It's fun—this spontaneous, crazy, loud display. But when the formation is tight, and the sing-song cadence is cleanly enunciated, and each foot of my classmates hits the pavement in step at the exact same moment, then, and only then, it becomes glorious. The sense of oneness combined with singleness of purpose and intention—my favorite moments in the police academy.

In this measured momentum, it's easy to forget the guy who's dumber than dirt, or the Hispanic older guy who thinks I shouldn't be elected class captain because I'm female. It's easy to forget the silly female who steals another cadet's boyfriend or tries to lay every cute visiting faculty by careful deployment of her pouting lips.

Yes, the foot-pounding formation erases individual strengths and weaknesses, flaws and imperfections.

Instead, we become one synchronized unit capable of right decisions, right actions, and thin-blue-line camaraderie. Does anyone else in the class feel this? I never ask. I don't need to know. My need is to keep this tiny secret controlled and contained inside myself.

No, I don't let my guarded secret erase my knowledge of the individual personal flaws I've seen in other cadets. Nothing can erase bad conduct—stealing boyfriends or husbands, lying to pass tests. But the coming together for a common purpose—such as these grueling late-night runs after sprinting up and down seven flights of stairs several times—is an almost transcendent confirmation of my understanding of law enforcement's mission. By living up to our sworn duty as police officers we can accomplish something bigger and better than our own uniquely selfish, private goals. Together, we can serve and protect—just like the mottos say. Although, many cadets laugh at the mottos. Sure, they want to do the job, but are already too cynical to buy-in to the official B.S. Those cadets see how unforgiving the streets are and how tough you must be to survive. My choice is to believe both sides—the heroic and the jaundiced. After all, these apparent contradictions exist in every job, every bureaucracy, all systems of human relationships. I suspect it will take years of willful living to accommodate both ends of the spectrum while figuring out my own unique path through the paradoxes. But I believe I can do so, and this belief keeps me whole.

After jogging, we wind up back beneath the overpass. Our DI instructs us to line up with plenty of space between ourselves in each row. Apparently, it's time for pushups—the male kind that require my body to be a solid plank of muscle supported only by bent toes and palms of hands. I've trained for this for months—just as I've pounded countless sawdust running trails in Memorial Park and innumerable concrete streets early in the morning and late at night. But even with months of preparation, pushups drive the gravel on the asphalt into the meat of my palm. It takes every ounce of strength during the final pushup when we hold our bodies in form, up from the ground, for two minutes. It's a question of simple endurance. I feel the burning from protracted straining flood my main muscle groups. But, you know what? I won't give up. No matter what—I won't break my form before the DI yells, "On your feet."

Maybe, I'm downright hard-headed. Stubborn, in fact. This internal drive is based on much more than the obvious fact that I'm class lieutenant and need to set a good example. What I want most is to show the guys in my class that females can be in just as good physical shape as the males. In fact, I'm so bound by my own ideas of equality—not uniformity—between the sexes that I've already begun to chafe at the women in this academy class who seem to regard themselves as merely ornamental. Who can't be bothered to get physically fit—those girls who giggle at everything. Females can be as serious about being a patrol officer as men are—I know this—I live it out.

And, you know what else is critically important to me? That every academy experience somehow makes me a better cop. Really, that's all I care about. One day I'll be out on the streets and I'll need every resource at my command—because every officer does. There will be those moonlit 0300-hours traffic stops when every male in a car of six outweighs me by 150 pounds, and no back-up is available. There might even be—as for Gomez—the traffic stop when the passenger in the front seat exits unexpectedly screaming, sprinting with a raised hatchet going straight at the police officer's skull. That's what all these pushups, chinups and jogging are about—making me a better cop. This is the only ruler I use.

*   *   *

The gray industrial carpet in my bedroom was chosen by prior owners who liked drab, designer colors. My duty belt and keepers lie on it, and next to them my unloaded gun. Each night, I practice drawing a hundred times before I go to bed. I do this because something like 85% of firefights happen within three yards of the cop involved. To "rock and lock"—the preferred and most efficient stance for dealing with deadly force at this short range—your forearm should be parallel to the ground. Achieving this perfect geometry requires 10,000 draws to create the muscle memory. I practice on my own this way no matter how exhausted I am, trying to reach the 10,000 before I must qualify with my firearm.

This bedroom used to be occupied by my husband, as well. The man now lives a couple miles away. I rarely think of him. Policing, learning to be a cop, has crowded him out of my mind. There's so much to absorb: Penal Code, Code of Criminal Procedure, how to make a traffic stop, types of sexual predators, crime scene preservation and analysis, domestics, how to shoot, how to handcuff, how to deliver a baby. The list is endless. My husband and I have been arguing for several years over my desire to go into policing. He says he isn't scared I'll get hurt—and I believe him. No, his aversion is more fundamentally self-centered than that. He's been a visual artist, a natural rebel against social order, all his adult life. He can't bear the thought of living with an enforcer of rules, a cop—society's supposed blunt tool against the presumed innocent. Now I wonder if he unconsciously knew he could never compete with the sheer adventure and blatant allure of learning how to survive on the streets.

I don't miss him as I lie between cool sheets waiting for sleep. The men I meet in policing have an energy and drive that is an unanticipated relief after years of listening to my husband's polemics on the leading twentieth-century French Deconstructionists. Yes, I had the education and the smarts to follow the discussions, but inwardly I rebelled against the need to make life so complicated, so brittle and joyless. Both my fellow male cadets and the working cops I'm now around are pleasantly uncomplicated. But uncomplicated doesn't mean inept or lacking in the IQ department. These are men who set goals, then work until they are accomplished. These are men who possess worlds of practical knowledge and use it. The exact placement of lube on handcuffs? *No problem*. How to ascertain the location of a structure's electrical ground? *Look over here, kid.* Figuring out the initial POI (point of impact) for a three-car pile-up with bodies ejected through windshields in the rain? *This is what you do first.* What's more—these men are willing to stand up for what they believe—just like me. Without fanfare, without making a lot of money, without becoming a hero—these are the men who know right from wrong and will stand up to protect society's innocents from being smashed by the criminals. These men don't stand on the sidelines and annotate essays. They are committed to action. This is profoundly fascinating to me after years of intellectual pursuits as the wife of a European intellectual.

I feel freed by the priorities of these future cops and the cops I date. Hot food (when possible). Great sex. Occasionally, a few cold beers and an evening dancing two-step. All this makes sense to me. I can do this.

I still think of those academy floors and walls as the silent witnesses to our single-purposed months of training. The insistent yellow brightness of the restroom tiles was only one of the backdrops to our private desperations and desires. For me, the tiles were witnesses to self-enforced discipline and steely devotion to becoming "the man." Downtown's deserted nighttime streets, without even the flickering of beer-sign neon, were yet another type of silent spectator to our ardent career hopes. The broken asphalt under steel trusses where we held push-up form until it felt like our lower backs would break was yet another backdrop. Certainly, the most credible testimony of our resolve would be given by the seven flights of unforgiving cement stairs we ran in nightly formation as the DI chased us in his pristine black sneakers, yelling threats of what he'd do to us if he caught us: *You'll bend for twenty-five. Right here, right now. Hustle up. Hustle up.*

We cadets were all colors, all body types, all ages. For some, like me, marriages on the brink already, crumbled. For some, again like me, the love of police work became stronger than any previous love. Some dated a smarter cadet only until the exams were done and passed. Some would die before telling a lie. One guy cheated to pass an exam, and was turned in by those cadets who knew.

All we were certain of was that we were on the road. Some of us might get killed, some of us might get injured. Some of us would be lucky—like the officer in the DI's story whose chest was stitched by automatic fire, but who sat up in the ambulance smoking a cigarette on the way to the ER. Some of us would be unlucky, or stupid, or find law enforcement something other than what we had hoped it would be. We all expected to have our hearts broken—whether by the job or by a wife/husband/lover—and we knew we were tough enough to survive. I knew it would not be easy, but I knew, just as surely, that I would persevere.

As graduation day approached, I felt a new urgency in every push-up, chin-up, or long mile on dirty asphalt jogging, spitting and sweating. "Soon" became my prayer; "soon" became my promise-to-self—even though there were no assurances of what the future held. But I had to keep up my spirits, so I repeated inside my head: Soon I'll have a job in a real police department. Soon I'll have my own uniform, be commissioned, be out on the streets. Soon, soon, soon.

Chapter Four

Eventually, there I was in the training corporals' small office with my cohort at my first police department, all four of us hired on the same day: two males, two females. We each had already made it downstairs to the respective male or female locker rooms to find the right-sized trousers and shirts. Our assigned FTO (field training officer) that day had already opened the long, narrow closet holding racks of shirts, trousers, rain coats, jackets, dress hats, holsters, keepers, and gun belts. He had rifled through small drawers to find the correct brass for each one of us.

Each piece of clothing and brass issued to us is recorded—all part of our responsibility to our agency. When we leave employment here, we'll have to return it, or our final paycheck will be lightened by its cost. I'm too excited to care, plus I'm good at keeping track of things. I'll make sure my brass and badge will have their own box, their own velvety resting place, adjacent to my other jewelry—like the thin gold band I no longer wear—in their own ornate box.

I've lost more for the privilege of wearing this new "jewelry" than I care to think about in daylight. The silvery, squared-off, military symmetry may not be decipherable to most civilians, just as it wasn't to me, at first, but I don't care. My brass is emblematic of my calling, my utterly unpredictable vocation to be a cop. I will love putting it on my shirt each morning carefully and lining it up in its square and shiny, metallic symmetry.

The corporal continues issuing our equipment. He coaches us through optimal placement of the items on the gun belt. My waistline poses a particular problem: it is very small, only 26 inches. There is barely room for magazine holder, holster, flashlight ring, baton ring, handcuff case, and radio holder. There's an optional separate, small black rectangular pouch that snaps shut, resembling an envelope, for carrying a set of plastic gloves in case of frisks or medicals, but on my gun belt that's hopeless—not enough circumference. My gloves will have to go in the back left trouser pocket.

Now that we're, at least, dressed like cops, we're herded down the long-carpeted hallway into the Chief's small conference room.

As we stand around the chipped wooden conference table, we look around. I think about everything I've left behind: the corner office in a gleaming high-rise downtown, the Italian designer high heels and sleek handbags, a trendy art scene's social status. A salary three or four times more lucrative. The marriage that promised so much and destroyed both of our hearts in the smash-up.

The Chief rushes into the rectangular room where we are standing, lined up on only one side of the table as our corporal ordered us. The Chief is serious, as he should be. He pauses and raises light blue eyes to each of us. He's probably hoping we'll succeed, while also thinking about the decades-long parade of rookies he's seen in his career. Some dead, some fired, some retired.

The oath—we repeat the words with our right hands raised after the gray-suited Chief says them—goes too fast for me. There's no thunder and lightning. No bugles. Only a hard-worn, seen-better-days-needs-a-refinish wooden table whose edge presses into our thighs. Gray industrial carpet. My uniform shirt scratches, and the new gun belt with its gear is heavy.

Yet despite all these typical low-bid, bureaucratic details, I've married myself to a duty I'll try to embrace with everything I possess—my mind, my heart, my pride and honor. And yes, with my body. I've pledged myself to the state of Texas and all its people. Whether they like me or not; whether I like them or not, I will die for them without stopping to think why.

What I can't yet realize is that my soul has indeed been transformed. The raising of the right hand and the formal words were the external signs of the profound paradigm shift that has been years in the making—becoming a protector. (Cops call themselves "the sheep dogs.") We are the ones who stand up for those who cannot stand up for themselves; the ones who protect the sheep from the sharp-toothed wolves always ready to devour the unsuspecting.

The mantle of responsibility isn't light on my shoulders, nor should it be. I wonder if the others in the room with me feel that same way. I want to ask but know that this would be an unacceptable intrusion—especially to the guys. Plus, I've been around enough men in my life to know that when they're embarrassed about taking something seriously they lapse into banter. Everything becomes a joke.

Tomorrow morning I'll show up for roll call. My boots will be perfectly shined. My hair is already cut to Regulation length. No rings, bracelets, or necklaces will adorn my person. The velvet-lined box where my brass slept all night will be empty. I'll feel awkward, a little nervous, but I won't show it. The stiff blue rayon shirt will still be itchy and hot. Every shift will be a thousand and one trials and tests rolled into the unpredictability of calls-for-service with their complainants, suspects, witnesses, and evidence. Thousands of opportunities to screw up as I'm trained to live up to departmental standards and protocols.

But today . . . today, elation reigns, guarded inside the fortress of heart. This is my secret—this satisfaction in taking the oath of office.

Before leaving the station today lugging all our new gear, we rookies stand together in the small upstairs office under the white asbestos tiles. We've talked enough among ourselves, when the supervisors are gone, that I know we're all dead serious about learning this job, then doing it well. One guy does joke about taking the oath, another razzes those of us who were so serious. It's okay. Their humor doesn't faze me. I am a cop in my heart and guts—where it counts.

Section Two

My Work Week

The only people whose clocks tick with mine are the other police officers on my shift. Our bedside tables probably hold the same $12.99 el-cheapo version of alarm clock from Walgreen's—a back-up to our cell-phone alarms. We mash the buttons on the clock down with blunt-nailed fingers still dirty from a previous shift and groan when the buzzer goes off—always too soon.

At work, we S/O (sign-on) on the radio each shift within roughly two minutes of each other, already hearing in the brief radio transmissions, each other's mood, level of stress, lack of sleep. I hear all this and more in the other officers' words—just as the guys I work with hear it in my own voice's timbre, tone, pitch, tightness. I diagnose each voice's amount of pissed-off-ed-ness, or stress-induced-by-supervisors, or marriage-trouble. There's also the ADA-dropped-charges blues, or worse yet, unfounded-complaint-filed-by-asshole-who-hates-cops. It's all there—in each voice, including my own, no matter how hard I, or they, try for an absolute monotone, that completely non-committal enunciation of unit numbers and location. If we were lucky, we had a few minutes to congregate in the station's parking lot to visit before the shift but, most of the time, calls are already stacked up. After signing out a hand-held, we race to our shops already planning the driving route to the first address, already praying it's simply a report call and not a call requiring an arrest early in the shift.

After working a full shift, we'll still be in sync time-wise as we go O/D (off-duty) on the radio within that same two-minute window of time. Our voices will be thick and gravelly with exhaustion and we'll share angry or sad outrages in low tones in the parking lot before we go home to try to sleep. We'll talk with each other about what we can't tell civilians, even if we sleep with them. We realize that, mostly, they love us; we don't expect them to understand us. They can't; they don't do the same job.

Each shift will progress in the same fashion, until, at the end of the work week, I will have five uniforms (shirts and trousers), five white T-shirts, five pairs black socks, and five pairs of underwear to launder. The only difference in the guys' and my dirty-clothes baskets is that my undies are black and theirs are white. Oh, yes—there's another crucial tie-breaker. My laundry includes bras.

Adjusting to the new work schedule when I was first assigned to Patrol wasn't that difficult, although I noticed the resultant social cost—that incalculable price that reverberated through my life. When I was no longer available for weekend parties, for fund-raising, for barbeques and cocktail hours, I no longer saw my friends or even my immediate family. Even though I had anticipated, even looked forward to, being out of sync with most of downtown society when I took on blue-collar work, I don't think I quite understood the practical isolation of sleeping when everyone else works or working when everyone else sleeps. This is one of the types of true loneliness in policing. A practical, daily reality for which there is no fix, no tonic strong enough to obliterate. After a while, it becomes a source of strength—yet another hurdle you make it over, that eventually winds up defining you because it seeps into your blood and identity. But you must make it through the loneliness until the isolation becomes your own food, your own unleavened bread—something you ingest to generate the energy required to work and work well through every shift.

For instance, I knew the "Friday" of my work week would not be on an actual Friday. (No new-hire in a police department gets weekends off.) I also had anticipated—as every rookie does—that I'd be placed on the worse shifts with the hardest sergeants, usually people who were promoted too early or for the wrong reasons and whose insecurities surfaced as a wishy-washy approach to supervision.

Prior to being a police officer, I'd always had a primary job that was salaried and safe. In those corporate jobs, I could, and often did, work long weekday hours and Saturdays. Yet, the unremitting hours at a desk in a pristine high-rise downtown were ten-thousand light years away from policing's grueling hours. Law enforcement's shift work with its numbing volume of calls-for-service, continuous physical demands, and hyper-vigilance took all of me. Corporate work, my specific skills in accounting and programming, had merely required a good brain and patience, a few social skills (not many), and a stylish wardrobe—that was it.

In sharp contrast, policing required everything inside and on the surface of me. All my equipment had to be in working order and well maintained. My uniform, posture, haircut had to convey competence and professionalism. My mind had to be focused and logical. At the downtown job, I had shelves of reference materials; in policing, I had what I could memorize—laws, departmental P&P (Policy and Procedure), the damn street names and geography of my beat. Both jobs took most of my time and brain power—certainly, at times, my equanimity. But only police work demanded the possibility of taking my life as well. That's a lot for $13.23/hour.

In addition, shift work automatically exerts its own unique tyranny on your off-duty time. Who else wants to party on a Tuesday night? For sure, not someone who has to get up at 5:00 a.m. the next morning and be at his desk by 8:00 a.m. for a full day at the law firm or architectural firm or medical office. So, forget dating a professional man. Who else wants to eat "dinner" at seven in the morning just before going to bed after eight or ten hours of work? The playing field isn't level; it's empty. Except for other cops.

I discovered this profound sense of disconnection was sometimes further enhanced by changes in my patrol shift schedule. Sometimes these hiccups are caused by court dates. After all, the courts are largely eight-to-five affairs, understandably in-step with corporate America but hugely out-of-step with most patrol police officers who often provide the majority of testimony in the cases. Sometimes schedule changes are caused by training mandates. Training, somewhat counter-intuitively, is an eight-to-five business as well. The night shift officers are required to work all night, then sit in eight hours of class, then sleep for several hours before going back to work at 2200 hours. Even the trainers don't hassle the night-shift hulks who doze off during class and walk pigeon-toed, gun belts drooping, between the tables at break, rubbing their blood-shot eyes. These are the exhausted guys who prop themselves up on muscular forearms in class, so they won't drop to the linoleum if they fall asleep.

After my first promotion I was required to be even more flexible as the corporals' schedules were flip-flopped often. I might work from 0800-1700 hours, so I could meet with my tall, kindly LT who only worked those hours. Then, I'd have to come back at 2200 hours and work until 0800 the following morning to train a rookie on deep nights. Sometimes I worked two eight-hour shifts back-to-back as the department was forced to hold-over a previous shift's officers because the next shift was short.

On these days, my eyelids burned, and my eyeballs felt like they swiveled against the hot grit of sandpaper left in the sun too long. And no, you can't make it up by sleeping more the following day. Sometimes the human body is too plain exhausted. Fortunately, my sense of duty always seemed to get me up out of the sheets when the alarm clock jangled its unwelcome message. Of course, my pay-per-hour was so low I needed the money, which was its own urgent incentive. In the semi-darkness after the alarm clock buzzed, I usually couldn't recall the day of the week or the time of day or night. I trusted that if I'd set the alarm, then I had to be at work. Once I had coffee I'd be awake enough to check my notes and see if this was a uniform or non-uniform day—if I was working patrol or undercover, on-duty or extra. I'd see if I was training probationaries or being trained, or any other of a host of assignments: bailiff, where 98% of the people are polite and the 2% of turds deliberately disobey every rule of the court; undercover, where everyone out there is nice because they don't realize I'm a cop; funerals, where everyone is stiff and uncomfortable—the men tugging dress shirts away from reddened necks and bobbing Adam's apples as they sweat in unfamiliar suits and rayon ties

What did I do, caught in the welter of arbitrary and sometimes unfathomable demands of shift-work with its broken rhythms of sleep time and its constant religion of self-sacrifice and exhaustion?

I sucked it up and in. I reminded myself that I chose to work blue-collar. I learned to sleep on demand—even if I needed to sleep sitting upright. I set two or three alarm clocks because, for the first time in my life, I could sleep through an irritating alarm clock buzzing for up to forty-five minutes. I slapped my face and pinched my cheeks to stay awake while driving to and from work. I learned that two hours free at home was enough time to shower, dry fire, shine my boots, and do laundry—maybe, eat too. I despaired of ever having enough sleep and one look at the red-eyed veteran officers I worked with told me that I would never again look well rested. I reminded the officers I worked with to drink enough bitter coffee from the Stop-and-Rob stores, and they reminded me. We all joked about needing caffeine to be available in IV form, but we also meant it.

And when I got to my "Friday"—which was usually a Tuesday or a Wednesday, I went home happy. For two twenty-four-hour periods, I would be out of the stuffy interior of a patrol car. At home, I'd gratefully peel off the uniform, the vest, the white tee, black socks and boots, then shower and be ready for—what?

I wouldn't know what to do with myself. My friends who still worked for corporations were in the middle of their work weeks. Most of my cop friends had different "Fridays." I would lie down on the smooth expanse of sheets I had been lucky enough to have time to wash that week. Every book I picked up contained fictions less thrilling than what I'd seen in the last twenty-four hours. Sure, I was special; I could be trusted to fulfill my mission for the people of Texas, for my supervisors, for my fellow officers. But, off-duty, I was on an island and no one was with me.

The only time I would feel right again was when I went back to work after those two days. Back to the same thankless job with its endless boredoms and dirt, with its tiny, stark terrors civilians rarely experienced or understood. Back to the job's specific calling with law enforcement's hidden rewards of intense camaraderie, sense of mission, and the fulfillments of justice and duty. Back to the job I chose of being a cop—the job I still love.

Old-time cops—the guys who have seen it all for decades—say that LE (law enforcement) is either in your blood, or not. If it is, then you can't give it up, no matter how old you are, no matter if you get injured or shot or attacked—like my patrol friend Andrew whose nose was broken six times by drunks in fist fights during ten years of working deep nights. Love of policing is like a separate strain of life inside of you—against all the odds, against all logic. You either have it or you don't, and it never leaves you. And if you do have it, you put up with all the troubles, the low pay, the lies in the newspapers, and the failures of the CJ (criminal justice) system.

In the beginning of my LE career, and even now, all these years later, I think the old-timers are correct. If your heart and mind and soul are those of a cop, then all the inherent difficulties of the profession—such as the screwed-up work schedules—become part of what makes you strong, part of what makes you and your fellow officers stay together as part of a team in the face of whatever mess and ugliness comes your way. In a sense, you might say that police officers' clocks never stop ticking in sync.

My Gender

I am sitting in the front passenger seat of a large white van at a gas station parking lot one county over. McBroom and I have been waiting several hours for prisoners from warrant raids to be brought to us for transport. So far, our prisoner count is zero. We fall into our routinely easy banter, the tit-for-tat kind of chain-yanking that cops in close quarters excel at.

Then, in reply to some stray observation, he launches into his reasons why females should be excluded from police work, fire-fighting, and the military—the great triumvirate of public service, where he's been employed throughout his entire life. I see his freckles color with his vehement rationalizations. Because I like him, I listen. I've never seen this side of him, and we've worked together on plenty of special assignments, like today's.

Moments like this don't often intrude into the already complicated mechanics of a working relationship in the field, moments that reveal startling glimpses of smoldering anger or prejudice, as well as humor and pluck. I prefer this out-and-out fessing up; better to meet attitudes head-on than try to grapple with unvoiced assumptions and the oily pastiche of false politeness. Besides, as I said, I like

McBroom; he likes me. He just doesn't like my gender in a uniform. It's that simple.

I listen carefully to McBroom's emphatic recitation of females' incompetence in the Army which then leads to a synopsis of all the female soldiers who asked him, as their military topography instructor at West Point, into their tents to examine their boot blisters during finals. These females were stark naked when he showed up, and, if he's to be believed, he promptly left the area after careful scrutiny of their *feet*.

All these years later he is still incensed over the fact that they thought they could bribe him with pussy to pass the map-reading course. As he continues talking, it's apparent that his anger is rooted in being asked by the females themselves to lie about their competence. I hear his disgust over the unnamed girls' assumptions that he had no professional standards that couldn't be measured by the length of his male parts, or erased by well-placed lubrication.

But, hell, who knows, maybe they just found his thick patch of strawberry-blond hair and blue eyes attractive? Some females might be attracted to a sturdy white boy with muscles honed by years of bull-riding and a genuine East Texas twang, especially with his Green Beret experience earned the hard way in the Southeast Asian rice paddies and jungles. He has clearly thought all of this through many times because he next points out that any female grunts who found him genuinely sexy would have tried to seduce him earlier in the training module. "Yeah, they just wanted to manipulate me, he fumes. In the field, they'd get somebody killed."

But today, *today* is what matters to me, and it's insanely important to convince McBroom that I have never slept with anyone to get anything—especially in law enforcement where rumors of scandal fly faster than the speed of light. His belief that a female cannot make the grade on her own ability, but must resort to sexual bribery is archaic to me, but to him, and to so many others in policing, it is a reality shored up by disastrous examples like the military story he has just related. I hear myself say the words, "McBroom, I've never slept with a man to get something career-wise," but I know he doesn't believe me. He can't. There is no way for light to penetrate the blinders surrounding this logic: Females are incompetent; I am a female; therefore, I am incompetent.

I understand these unfortunate attitudes because I've seen the same disastrous deviations from accepted professional standards by some female police officers: the female from another agency that attended a LE training wearing painted-on jeans, a black push-up bra, and a light pink blouse unbuttoned deep into the middle of her chest, or the female patrol officer who took bottles of nail polish into her cruiser to paint her fingernails on-duty, between calls-for-service. Her specialty, glittery pink.

Sometimes the assumption is that women aren't serious about a career in police work. A female recruiter and patrol veteran at LAPD once told me that the primary reason females wanted to work there as cops was "to get a husband." I'm guessing those girls wear lots of pink too with black, lacy bras that show every detail through translucent blouses while attending mandatory LE training. I call these other female officers "dolls" and wonder how they got past Recruiting with their heavy makeup, long fingernails, and calculated fashion-model prettiness. The women who are dedicated to being competent police officers (especially patrol officers)—pretty or not—don't like or understand the dolls and their priorities. Probably, vice versa as well.

Sometimes the assumption is that women can't be effective in a grimy blue-collar job. This is especially true within the sacred trinity of public service: military, fire, police—beyond which nothing worth doing exists for those of us called to public service. Careers in medicine or education might be better accepted by most parents, but when it comes to action, risk, danger, *proving yourself a man*, there is *only* this trinity. And, if you are a female like me, who craves danger on the job, then you will have to be ten times better than any male. You'll have to pretend you don't know you're usually better than most of the males you work with, sometimes smarter, faster, more detail-oriented, more tactically sound, have better hand-writing, smell better, make more arrests, clear more cases, write more citations. And remember, if any of them notices, then they'll probably hate you for it.

It's hard on both sides of the fence: the men who were raised with ideas about females being less strong than men—physically and emotionally; the women who want to be as much of a "man" as the men are. For me, there's never been a question that I can do what any man can do emotionally. Poise under pressure has been one of my attributes since childhood, and LE training has reinforced it to an art. Yet often the assumption is that women are more prone to over-reactions and are too sensitive to work well on scenes that involve massive amounts of blood, random severed body parts, and hysterical crime victims and bystanders.

Thank goodness, there are now so many female police officers who dispel the old-fashioned attitudes. For instance, at a book signing, a woman who bought a poetry book of mine about policing, told me that her niece had been the police supervisor in charge of the scene at Columbine, and the first unit on the scene. She kept it together at the school and did her job amid the carnage, but later left policing because of the emotional havoc wrecked on her by working that scene. Whenever I remember that story, I say a prayer for that young woman who left the career she loved and in which she had invested years of effort and sacrifice. I wish that more civilians could understand and appreciate the toll that we police officers pay to do our jobs well—as that young woman did.

In fact, there's a new category of female police officer unofficially called the "Dangerous Doll." These elusive warriors are the strong, powerful women who, in carefully drawn make up and beautiful shades of matching lipstick, plus hair gel, manage to wipe up the floor with any criminal who attacks them, then at the end of shift turn in paperwork so complete, so impeccable, that their sergeants want to clone them to populate the entire shift and ditch all the male officers.

However, until there are more Dangerous Dolls in police departments, it's not only the fellow officers that can perceive female police officers as ineffective. I've seen a convenience store tape of an aggravated robbery-in-progress where the B/M (black male) suspect chose not to shoot a female cop who entered the store a few minutes behind him and couldn't see his gun because of where they each stood because (he later stated) "she wasn't a threat to me." You see, even the criminals can be prejudiced—although, in this case, it saved the female's life.

A crucial anatomical difference, vitally important in LE, is the size-strength differential between men and women. In fact, back in the sixties and seventies when women were pressing hard to be allowed to become patrol officers, the research showed some counter-intuitive results related to the size of the officer and the probability of potential attack by suspects. The results showed that people prone to attack police officers were no more prone to attack smaller officers than bigger; conversely, they were not less prone to attack larger officers. This research opened the door for knocking down the height and weight requirements—which had eliminated both smaller males and almost all females from applying successfully to police departments for jobs other than baby-sitting female juvies or "jail matron" (as it was called) in a lock-up for adult females.

So, decades later there's no surprise in acknowledging that male police officers tend to be stronger than female officers, particularly when it comes to upper body strength. Look at the anatomy books. The clincher is whether the men *always think* they are better police officers because they are stronger. Silent attitudes vs. actual job performance. Hoisting yourself over a six-foot fence demands a strong upper-body physique; going into a local drug store after a bomb threat does not. I figure all I can do is perform the job to the best of my ability. And, yes, that does include being physically fit to maintain my own strength. Each officer—male and female—bears this responsibility.

One of my best male friends in policing says, "I protect female cops I work with as if they are my little sisters." Some female cops would be insulted by this attitude—I'm not because I know that he acknowledges female officers as his equals or betters. I've heard him advise rookies, "we're all in this together—we all bleed red" when they ask how to relate to female officers on the streets. This is also the same guy who related to me with genuine admiration welling up in his amazed voice how he watched, as he rolled up on a scene, the primary unit, a female cop, exit her vehicle to deal with a drunk wife-beater. As dirtbag was swinging to hit her, she grabbed him, put him on the ground, rolled him over, then handcuffed him before my friend could even exit his own car. *Amazing. I was her back-up, and she didn't even need me. And I'm a foot taller than she is. She had it totally handled.* His attitude is now more prevalent than ever as female combat vets become cops. Needless to say, they operate at a very low simmer. No boiling over. The ultimate in poise.

There is no equality between men and women officers on the streets. Men are definitely stronger; women are meaner.

Men can be disastrously short-tempered; women communicate better. Men are better initially at B.S. and sustain it longer; women carry grudges and never stop hating someone once they've started. Men tend to like straightforward feedback. There's great freedom in being able to slap someone on the bicep and tell him to quit being a jerk. He'll usually grin and stop his irritating behavior—because he knows he was being a dick. I adore this freedom. Easier work dynamics, less stress. I certainly never had this easy communication or compliance in the corporate world's clean-carpeted offices or the university's PC, back-stabbing corridors.

Not surprisingly, I prefer working with men. Men are less neurotic, less backbiting—at least, out in the open. Every time I hear the story of another female cop who is sleeping with fellow male officers, or being a cry baby in a supervisor's office, I feel personally betrayed. The burden of diminished expectations from all the male officers increases by one more brick, sealed by the mortar of whispered "I told you so's" that I'll never hear out loud, but will have to attempt to overcome by the sheer dint of reliable work product veiled in silence.

So, if you're another rookie female who wants to become a cop and come out on patrol with us, keep your mouth shut, your trousers zipped, and your nail polish at home. Here, everything is dead serious, even when we laugh at jokes you don't yet understand. And McBroom and I will continue laughing, even though I'll never convince him through logical conversation that I am that different kind of girl he can't fathom—a competent girl, with a badge, in tactical boots and trousers, with no designs on his manliness. A girl who doesn't wear fluffy dresses and is probably a better shot than he is. Meaner, too.

Bottom line, I like him; I'll cut him some slack. As he'll probably do for me, for exactly the same reason. I'd like to think it's our unconscious solution hammered out in crucibles like this one: prisoner transports and warrant raids, straight-faced briefings before deployments and exhausted de-briefings afterwards—hammered out in the only crucible that matters to both of us as cops: our daily work in the criminal justice system.

So, I grin at McBroom sitting on the driver's side of this huge elephant of a white van one county over. "Hey, McBroom," I say. "Quit being a dick, you know females are better than men at everything—don't you?" He laughs and shakes his head, looking through the windshield at a low flying bird against the summer-bright blue sky. The laugh lines, radiating out from his eyes, crinkle. "Yeah, that's what my wife says."

"Dead right, McBroom," I say. "Don't make me dope-slap you as a reminder."

Our Stories

Advice from more experienced police officers comes thick and fast. It's often couched in the stories told across scarred tables in the squad room. Maybe, across burning hot car hoods in the station's parking lot under scrappy shade from tall pines.

Cops love to tell stories; they love to hear them, often unconsciously training less experienced officers through an oral tradition combining tactical details and gallows humor. Every story begins, "I had this call-for-service," or "This call dropped. . . ." That's the moment of destiny when each officer collides with the unique welter of screw-ups inherent in every call-for-service. Cops know that if the situation could've been have handled by an ordinary citizen, then the call to the police would never have been placed. As a veteran patrolman told me early on, "Nobody *wants* you there—not really. Just sometimes they *need* you because they can't handle the situation on their own. By the time you arrive, things are already snarled up good."

Often, my writer's sensibility has thought that an entire novel would need to be written just to convey what's inside any single person at a scene. And don't forget, each scene has multiple actors—the reportee, the suspect, the crime victim, the witnesses, if any. Any of these categories may overlap—what if the suspect didn't commit the crime, but the reportee did? What if the witness committed the crime but is lying to throw suspicion on someone else? What if the officer's instincts tell him who committed the crime, but there is no physical evidence? What if a terrible moral injustice was done, but it's not illegal?

I never forget that each person will have his own reasons to lie or tell the truth—whether totally or partially. Each person will be hiding something that he doesn't want to tell—which may or may not be related to the crime I'm trying to investigate. Perhaps, some of these puzzling configurations of human behavior account for the startling popularity of criminal investigation shows on TV. Who knows? But something tells me that few of those avid watchers of cop and CSI shows really want to be crawling on their hands and knees in 110-degree weather through muddy, forested areas full of mosquitos looking for the scene of a sexual assault. The grimy realities of criminal investigation are thankless and often nothing more than fruitless. The only reward for those of us who do it is that justice, as defined by our legal system, will be served.

At times, a call-for-service has made me wish for the eloquence of a nineteenth-century Russian novelist. I've hungered for that impossibly high level of writing skill, so I could write, for instance, the storied nuances inside the exhausted posture of an elderly W/F trying to take care of a violent, mentally-ill adult daughter. This is the stuff of Dostoevsky and Chekov: the deadness in the mother's gray eyes, the forlornness that has reduced her skin to fragile, white tissue. The exhausted hopelessness stalking her days. But for me, this is also only one of the calls-for-service in a shift that has calls dropping every few minutes; a shift during which I will not get a lunch break and barely time to pee. A shift during which I will not have time to write even one sentence of the novel my heart tells me the mother deserves.

When I get home at the end of shift, I will be too exhausted to pen words to paper. I will unsnap keepers, lower my gun belt to the floor, and climb into the shower. I will pray that the penetrating greasiness left in the pores of my skin from peoples' lies and cruelty will wash down the drain. Don't you know that I will be grateful for the illusion of cleanliness from the hot water gushing from the showerhead? Cops take long showers—for a lot of reasons.

At the beginning of tomorrow's shift when I get back to the station to lug my black patrol bags into the shop, I will joke and listen to more stories. Maybe, tell a few of my own. After all, our lives as police officers are built around stories—other peoples' stories. In a peculiar way, we officers don't get to have our own personal stories, at least not on the job. Instead, we become the spine of hard bone around which other peoples' stories and lives will weave, sometimes suffocating us, sometimes merely forming a colorful tapestry of humorous bright threads.

It's this same humor that is often utilized in the stories cops tell each other, probably because it's the only on-duty relief cops get in dealing with the unpredictability, the brief splashes of terror, or deep-rooted, wasted tragedy of most human behavior we encounter. Not for nothing do cops also laugh at themselves—it's therapeutic, and necessary because there's nothing that's ever been written from the fictitious world of the imagination that comes close to what we see, do, and hear, day in and day out.

Here's a humorous example from the true-life career of Jeff, a patrol friend of mine. "My car-share worked deep nights; I worked evenings, so the car sat vacant during day shift. The lady living next to the substation fed throngs of stray cats. One winter morning when my car-share took his gear out of the car, he must've left a door open. A stray cat climbed in unnoticed. Understandable, because it was below freezing, and he'd had the heater on, so the car was toasty warm inside. When I came on-duty at 1400 hours, the entire inside of the car from windshield to MDT to seats to floorboards was covered in liquid-pissed-off-cat-shit. I couldn't even run any calls. I had to take it to be cleaned. For months, even years after, I would find catnip hanging from my rearview mirror or cat food cans in my mail drawer at the station." Yep, cops have long memories for the funny stuff.

Or another example from Scott, one of my FTOs later killed by a drunk driver while working extra: "This call dropped for a burglary of habitation in-progress. I got there—a huge house. Bedrooms in different zip codes. Three or four other units arrived including a K-9 unit and his dog. So, we're all searching through this house in the dark. All spooked, because there was an open door, and we didn't know where the bad guys were. We searched everywhere, and it checked clear. By that time, the homeowners arrived. We're standing in this big dish of a sunken living room, and, suddenly, the K-9—a German shepherd, a beautiful dog—coughs. A white feather floats out of his mouth. He keeps coughing and more feathers rise to the ceiling. Turns out that dog had eaten some expensive bird on a perch in the sunroom. A white cockatiel. Man, those people were pissed, and the PD had to pay for the bird."

Then, there are those stories that are just plain funny and sad, simultaneously. Those moments that hold a magnifying glass against the futile malice inside human behavior when people get cross-ways. "There was this investigator, and he ate lunch every day at his desk. Made a big production out of it. Brown paper bag. Folded neatly—a new one every day. Saltines in a baggie. Can of tuna fish in that crinkly brown bag. He'd take the can of tuna into the kitchen and open it, then come back to his desk and eat the tuna with his crackers. He'd been going through rough times in his marriage. Maybe, by this time, thinking about separation or divorce. Then, we noticed something. The can of tuna wasn't tuna no more. We didn't know whether to tell him or not. Finally, somebody said, 'Jeremiah, what you eating?' 'Tuna. This here is tuna, boy.' 'I don't think so, Jerry. Look at the can.' He looks at the can and just about throws up. 'That bitch,' he says. That's it—just two words: 'That bitch.' You see, it was a can of cat food. She'd switched to get back at him."

So, this is how we police learn from each other on the streets. No detail is too small, no location description too long, no crime scene too gruesome for us to learn from, as we hear the story. We listen up to all the stories—stories, both funny and dark, distilled from experiences with criminals, crazies, regular folks, and assorted people bent on no good. We memorize everyone's story as we hear it. We memorize as if our lives depended on it, and they very well may. We become walking encyclopedias of other peoples' crushing sadness and calculated meanness, sometimes of their stupidity and naivete, sometimes of their triumphs of the human spirit in the face of grief, loss, and the inexplicable.

To survive, we laugh when we tell those stories. Humor is part of our armor—part of how we prepare to do the job we were hired to do. Then afterwards, we'll share that story with other officers who will either understand already or, maybe, learn something new, then one day in the hard future, understand.

Knife-Girl

Right after I was assigned to a new beat, a call dropped one evening for a domestic between two sisters. The mom was screaming into her kitchen phone at the dispatcher. A butcher knife. No injuries.

Two of us showed up—a Corporal and me. He had put his numbers on the call, so he took the lead. The sisters were identical twins, sixteen years of age—just shy of the legal definition of an adult in the state of Texas. Their eyes were unusually large and dark. Objectively, I'd say the girls could've been beautiful: pale skin, those haunting and expressive eyes, a pretty mouth. But the way we were seeing them was no good—angry, hateful, not a lick of common sense between them. The only thing they knew was that tonight they despised each other and wanted to take some action on it. Deadly action.

The twin who had taken off after her sister with Momma's kitchen knife had wrists too thin for the smallest circumference on my cuffs. So, I sat her down uncuffed on the entranceway's stone tile and let her play with her new puppy. The pup was short-haired and beguiling in the soft way of bungling puppies. My twin kissed and petted him constantly as he roamed in and out of her small, cross-legged lap.

As the corporal unwound the facts of the incident, he decided both the girls need to go to jail given the types and amounts of provocation before the butcher-knife chase up the beige-carpeted stairs, but the ADA refused charges. That left us to find a cooling-off location for one twin. Mom called a female family member she trusted to come over to pick up the twin I now thought of as "knife-girl."

I walked upstairs with her to her bedroom to watch her pack an overnight bag—standard routine, especially on domestics where it's not safe to leave anyone alone to access a weapon. Her normal, residential track-housing door and door jamb had one highly abnormal feature—a sturdy padlock and hasp. It had been removed and re-installed several times leaving an ugly mess of small wooden splinters. When I asked her about it, she said she had to keep family out of her room "otherwise things got stolen."

With the dark maroon carpet as background, countless articles of clothing were scattered around the room. No furniture. She pulled a tote bag from the closet and stuffed random clothes off the floor into it, being careful to choose several pairs of frilly, colorful, see-through panties.

Back downstairs, the corporal had already given everyone all the required legal forms for a domestic and patiently listened to the mom's self-righteous rendition of the family's history for the last fifteen years. My shorter listening period only caught me up on the family's latest fiasco—a do-it-yourself interior paint job of the upstairs that explained why the living and dining rooms were full of standing mattresses angled against every wall and on top of couches.

The girl gave her puppy a gentle good-bye kiss on his black nose, then left with the family member. Neither one of them looked back.

The corporal's weary observation to me as we walked down the sidewalk while the girl rode off: "We'll be seeing her again."

* * *

A year or so later I was dispatched to the same address in the late afternoon of a sunny weekday. Of course, I recognized the house. That's part of what cops memorize—which calls drop, at which locations. You'd be surprised how many houses hold unhappiness, how many calm facades behind trimmed bushes hide the illegal and the unspeakable. The mom wanted to press charges for theft against knife-girl for unauthorized use of a credit card.

The girl was present, and they both were screaming at each other. Many snatches of the shouting match between the girl and her mother sounded routine. Not that the words weren't both passionate and spiteful, but the long list of fault, guilt, and blame took in things that should have long ago healed, like the Dad's decision to walk out when the girl was a toddler.

Finally, the mom backed out of filing charges for the credit card abuse. I had figured that she would, for even to a non-parent like me, it was evident that this young, skinny, and beautiful daughter was loved by her mom with fierce attachment.

Through all the crying and yelling—the daughter pacing restlessly from the kitchen into the dining room, then back again, as if the wake of her energy could stir up something new—the daughter decided to move out. She was an adult by law now, and neither her mom nor I could make her live at home.

Part of what I learned by listening to them was that the girl had recently started working at Rick's, a gentleman's cabaret. The wadded-up dance outfits she packed into her cheap suitcase were barely as big as my fist. They were elasticized, but it was obvious they didn't stretch to cover much.

I remembered something one of my first police mentors, who'd been the captain over Vice for years, had said almost ten years earlier: "The only females those girlie clubs can get that are stupid enough to take their clothes off and dance naked in front of strangers are very young. They get'em young and get'em full of booze and drugs. They're too young to see how stupid they are."

Part of the money knife-girl had stolen from her mom was for cigarettes. The ADA had refused charges on a small bit of marijuana the mom had found in the girl's padlocked bedroom and produced with a flourish for me to see. The tad of softness that knife-girl had previously displayed towards the puppy was gone, as were the pup and the other sister. I didn't doubt the girl would wind up eventually like her mom—crying at a cheap kitchen table, every horizontal filled with half-consumed boxes of food and diet drinks, rafts of coupons, disposable neon cigarette lighters, and wadded-up paper towels. A cigarette burning up her loneliness in huge gulps of smoke into lungs that were already laboring.

No track marks on knife-girl's arms, yet.

As the girl sorted through dirty laundry to get the clothes she wanted to take, her mountain of a mother got up from the kitchen and yelled her goodbye: "One day . . . one day you're going to be like me—fat and ugly. Right now, you have that cute, tiny body. You think you're something else because all the guys are after you. But you'll see. One day you'll look just like me and remember today."

Every inch of Mom shook with the sobbing. She was right; she knew it and I knew it. The girl rolled her dark eyes to the ceiling, thrust the dirty clothes into her laundry basket with a few weary stuffed animals, and walked out the front door, balancing everything in scrawny, unsteady arms.

One Woman

The dull, hard sheen of summer's afternoon sun on the roadway hurts my eyes, although they are shaded behind metallic aviators. My next call-for-service spreads the ache from my tired eyes through my entire skull. Even the blood pumping through my brain begins to hurt. Squinting doesn't help.

Family violence always increases a headache because this type of call is so stressful, so unpredictable to work. Added to the decades-long march of annual statistics that all cops know—the probability of getting killed or injured on a family violence call is high—is the complexity of human dynamics that makes these calls so difficult. It's not just the swirling desperation that runs at a fever pitch, but the bitter residuals after years of manipulation, frustration, and anguish. Stir these together, shake with a little alcoholic beverage or a tad of illicit, mind-altering chemical substance, then layer with a perceived family crisis, and you have a family violence call-for-service.

I memorize the address at the same time my brain figures out the fastest way to get there—just in case the CAD (Computer-Aided Dispatch) system hiccups into wrong geography, as sometimes happens. I replay the details recited by the dispatcher: no known weapons, unknown drug or alcohol, suspect not on-scene, female caller, three children on-scene. Although I've sat in casual, apartment living rooms with other cops off-duty and laughed at the film industry's inaccurate depictions of police procedures, I can imagine a Hollywood camera in the patrol car with me. Is there a way to make the weary upholstered seat seem urgent and sexy? What camera angle will convey my competence and resolve? Is there a way to film the stream-of-consciousness that spools its nervous way through my brain?

Please understand me—I'm not nervous. It's my body that's nervous. My brain unrolls long lists of procedures, cautionary tales, tactical decisions, court cases, et cetera, that become an ominous movie of their own inside my head—the "What-If" game. Every police officer ambushed, stabbed, shot or beaten on this type of call flashes through my memory (especially the bald cop ambushed from behind with a hatchet cleaving his skull)—and for these exemplars I am grateful.

All these scenarios feed my readiness. There will be first contact with the caller and my assessment of the scene. Then I'll need time to interview everyone, assess evidence, figure out if I have a crime or not, and, if need be, take someone to jail. Then comes the crucial step of writing a good report and, perhaps, testifying in court.

No, there's no way, I think, that Hollywood could ever capture this onslaught of cautionary memories threaded with the hopes for going home uninjured, and the strong prayer for tactical smarts and, on top of it all, for somehow accomplishing the best thing for the family. No, Hollywood will never succeed at getting this right, although it tries and tries, always failing as it mistakenly focuses on sex and gore—as if the first could purchase immunity from the second, or is it the other way around in today's senseless postmodern world portrayed on the screen?

Meantime, I am driving as fast as departmental policy

will allow given the priority assigned to the call by Dispatch. Luckily, this call-for-service is on a street I have memorized so there's no delay in arrival. I careen around corners and keep my ear attuned to the dispatcher's updates. Listen for a unit to back me up, although today there's no one available. I'll be going in alone.

I do as other experienced officers have told me, particularly for domestics—do not park in front of the residence. Even though today I have broad, summery daylight with a bold blue sky, I follow every precaution. Daylight holds no promise of safety. I learned that lesson early from a policing mentor who began as an MP during the Vietnam era in West Germany. His base had a problem with German extremists shooting American soldiers in sunny morning daylight on deserted, flower-filled boulevards so beautiful they looked like a high-grade color postcard. As a civilian, years ago, I thought nighttime made killing easier, or, at least, more probable. Now, as a cop, I know when someone wants to kill, the amount of light doesn't stop him or her. The probability of extinction flourishes 24/7.

Walking up to the house from the side, I notify the dispatcher to hold the channel—standard procedure when an officer needs to make sure no one can hear the tell-tale police radio while he assesses. Plus, on this type of call, there's a good chance I'll hear people arguing, or yelling and screaming—all of which may become evidence or, at the least, a clue to what's really going on. There's only silence beneath the fluttering leaves of large trees. No car in the driveway. Cheap plastic bikes are overturned on the lawn. The lawn itself is ragged. No one has swept the front porch steps. Small, fluttering wisps of disintegrating paper cling to the front shrubbery in contrast to the surrounding manicured middle-class neighborhood.

I make sure I'm not located directly in front of the doorway when I ring the doorbell. Standing on the bare cement steps, I realize with brutal clarity that it's one of those moments when someone could kill me. Even though I've followed every tactical procedure mandated by my agency, even though I've made tactically sound decisions based on training films and Academy training—despite all these actions—in the next few seconds, anyone on the other side of the door could blast me with a shotgun, rifle, or handgun. That's the reality of my policing world. Maybe that is part of the rationale for the oft-repeated comment from civilians thanking police officers for being brave. I don't know. I wouldn't call my series of tactical decisions by that name. I'd simply say that each police officer has made peace with what might happen on the other side of that peeling, orange-painted wooden door, or any door. Once I knew what I'd be willing to die for, I didn't have to think of dying again. I was free to concentrate on the pragmatics: line of fire, tactical readiness, number of suspects, availability of backup, every small detail of sight, sound, color, and smell.

Today, however, I don't get killed. A W/F opens the door. She's a large woman, very large. Long, lank blonde hair that's received the same amount of attention as the overgrown, raggedy grass outside. The woman's mouth twists into what might be a grin—it's hard to tell. Inside her mouth is only a single yellowed tooth. It protrudes from her top gum, and it's grown downward about twice the regular length of a tooth. The remainder of her mouth is a railyard of gaping, pink depressions. She wears a tent of a printed cotton dress with no sleeves and more than one day's worth of stains down the front.

Now begins my time to listen and ask questions. I try to read the shorthand of her thin, tight lips, her stained top tooth. What are their secrets pertaining to this call-for-service? While she's talking, I scan her bare arms for signs of drug usage or bruises. I look carefully for defensive wounds: at her neck for signs of strangulations, at her eyes for the small knots of patterned blood—either from dope or petechial hemorrhage—and at her knuckles for bruises. I release the channel by telling the dispatcher to return to routine radio traffic. Tell the dispatcher I don't need backup. I've been here less than two minutes.

There are many questions: Why did she call today? What happened today? Last night? Where is her husband? Does he live here? How long has she lived with her husband? How many children? Their ages? Does he hit her, strangle her, pull the phone from the wall, slap her, cut her, burn her, kill or torture her pet/s, make her go without medical care, bite her? What are the husband's interactions with the kids? The list is endless because the human imagination for cruelty and humiliation is without limits for those who choose to abuse others.

I listen for a long time. I talk to the listless, blond-headed children whose bikes are scattered outside. They aren't unfriendly, but they don't smile and answer in monotones. Mostly, they are silent—three slender torches topped by straight hair and watchful, gray eyes. I try not to remember that the stats say most boys who grow up in households where the father abuses the mom will grow up to do so themselves—no matter how much they hated it at the time it occurred. It's important for me not to remember this depressing statistic because I want to have hope for every child I encounter—even on calls like this.

After extensive questioning, a telephone call to Child Protective Services and to the ADA, I am validated in my judgement that there is no crime here. Yes, the husband is a jerk. Yes, he does things that no right-minded woman with healthy self-esteem would allow a husband or boyfriend to do. But the particular actions she has described are not illegal, so I have to tell the woman goodbye. Besides, a crucial part of the CJ system is that there are always two sides to every story, if not eight or ten. That's why physical evidence is so important. Is she telling the truth? What is the husband's side of the story? Is there evidence to support one side or the other? I'll never find out unless the police are called back here again, and the fact pattern is different from today's.

Yet part of me wants to scold her—like an affectionate but stern grandmother might do—for putting up with an immature, selfish, son-of-a-bitch husband. Part of me wants to yell at her for getting herself in the position that she is in today—no job, virtually no education, no car for transportation, no income, bad health, and a depressing appearance. I want to yell at her for bringing three kids into this hopeless house with its dynamics geared toward humiliation and failure. Of course, I don't scold or yell. Instead, I wish her luck. I've already listened hard out of respect. I repeat the advice and repeat it once again hoping that it will give her some peace of mind and confidence. I give her phone numbers for social service agencies that might be better able than I to coach her into a better life. Phone numbers for women's shelters in case things spiral out of control in new ways; phone numbers for counselors for the kids. Even knowing she has no transportation to get to these places, I place the sharply printed black-and-white small information cards (handy for pockets) in her large, callused hands. She doesn't need to know that I've listened over and over again to similar stories on what feels like thousands of calls from both men and women whose lives have entered the Never-Never land of despair; the only emotional pain that matters to her is her own—as it would be for most people.

For years afterwards, as I drive by the two-story, red brick and white-lumber topped house, I think of that one tooth—the curving, yellowed bone. The sole survivor in a tortured mouth that I still see gaping in despair, as if she couldn't breathe, couldn't find air anywhere to replenish her.

That woman talked about how bad she looked. She apologized for it—as if my concern for her was rooted in appearance rather than the simple fact that she was another human being in distress. My guess would be that the husband reminded her often of her looks. In fact, one of her complaints about her husband was that he wouldn't give her the money to get false teeth when her others fell out. There was no point in me telling her his behavior was typical of control-junkies. No point in telling her that looks don't matter.

Even now, when I think of that curving arc of bony tooth, I find deep compassion for her. It doesn't do her any good, unfortunately, but upon it rests the same prayer I have for everyone I've seen on domestics who was abused, mentally or physically, by another—my prayer is that that person finds a way to escape safely. To heal in a profound way. The outcome I pray for is statistically improbable—I know that, but I continue praying because it is not *impossible*, only improbable. Sort of like me standing outside that peeling, orange front door, then against the odds, walking away intact and capable of going home at the end of a shift. A shift that has included plenty of sunshine, with its cheerful deceptions, and plenty of misery, with too few glimmers of transcendent healing for those hit hard on the tangled peripheries of life.

Kitchen Hungers

Tonight, I'm trolling for food at the station. I've just completed the prisoner search of another officer's female arrestee next door at the jail, and that means my excuse for being out of service is over. On the way to the back door and my patrol car sitting outside, I walk into the station's large kitchen. Maybe, I'll get lucky.

Almost all the kitchen's surfaces are gray: cabinets, countertops, linoleum. What isn't gray is dark brown or utilitarian stainless steel. The room is long on boredom; short on pretty. Bike patrol bicycles rest against one wall right next to the annual Christmas wreath and the box of plush teddy bears in pale colors.

Five coffee makers squat on the smudged countertop to the left of the sink: two Keurigs, a Black & Decker, a Cuisinart, an octopus of a contraption from Boyd's Coffee. Four digits on the Black & Decker flash an intermittent blue "1200" that no one in the station has bothered to set to the correct time. Tonight, I'm not willing to drink anything out of these machines, although I can remember other winter nights when hot and bitter was better than nothing at all. Those nights when my toes were numb despite thick-walled tactical boots and two pairs of wool socks. The nights when my entire foot was so cold it felt like a block of ice when I pressed it against the accelerator or brake.

But as much as I crave warmth, I don't need anything liquid. My stomach's desperation—sustained and insistent—is for food. Vasquez and I had planned to catch dinner together earlier—before calls stacked up and we had to run them back-to-back with no breaks—but, true to form, calls-for-service before our meet-time sent us spinning into different orbits. It is now hours later with reports stacking up—to be typed—and affidavits for citations to be completed. There's no way to go through a fast food drive-thru because nothing is open this late. His stomach is growling too, I bet, out there somewhere in the unfriendly darkness of cold concrete and dead lawns. He won't let anyone hear the hunger in his radio voice, but I know it's there in the pit of his stomach—just like for me.

In all the years I've worked out of this station I've never seen any of these coffee makers working during evening or night shifts. Usually day shift makes and drinks coffee—that's when the LTs, captains, and chiefs are here. They are the ones who have desks to keep those stained coffee cups, stacked in the cabinets, stable. The rest of us—in patrol cars—resort to getting our coffee in the flimsy Styrofoam cups from convenience stores. I've heard stories about a large cup of scalding coffee spilled in a lap as an officer maneuvers with burned thighs driving to a Code One call-for-service. These dramatic tales of masculine pain have convinced me to play it safe. I hesitate to slurp even cold drinks in the patrol car. Let other officers piss off their car-share on another shift by leaving a sticky puddle of sugary soft drink in the seat or on the floorboard. Too bad the cars' cupholders aren't designed for anything but short cups.

Next to the coffee makers is one tall coffee carafe with a press handle at the top for dispensing liquid. Below a table next to the countertop and refrigerator is a five-gallon ice-tea metal carafe on the linoleum floor. I'd like to be convinced by the colorful logo and idyllic picture on the front of it, but iced tea, in my mind, equates to leisure, and leisure doesn't happen in police work. Boredom, yes—at times—but a souped-up, anxious boredom—not leisure, not a summer-grasshoppers-on-the-lawn-and-hammock kind of leisure. The ice tea must have been for a fundraiser or a meeting with citizens. Something that requires plenty of social skills and handsome faces—something for the higher-ups.

I scan for any free food that's been left on the long center tables in the kitchen's midsection. The protocol's shorthand is that food left there, and there alone, can be eaten by anybody. Donations from LE supporters, gifts, even leftovers from other personnel receive this treatment. I don't care what the food is, if it doesn't involve liver, sushi, and isn't blood-meat raw. I am so hungry that I would even eat chocolate, one of my least favorite things in the world. However, I'm not desperate enough to open the packets of ketchup or mustard in one of the drawers lying next to the rusted can openers in the second drawer to the right of the sink. Not yet, anyway.

On the long tables in the center of the room are a couple of plates of crumbs with the plastic wrap half-way pulled off. One set of crumbs is chocolate and looks to have been brownies. The other set of crumbs looks to have been sugar cookies. I consider licking a finger and pressing it into the sugar-cookie crumbles, and my stomach growls at the prospect of nourishment. But I can't. Who knows what else has been pressed against that plate or how many hours or days it has sat here? Sometimes wives of other patrol officers give their husbands a plate of goodies to bring to work, and they're placed on the long tables. But I'm too late—typically, by night shift, everything has been devoured. The portion of my brain that yearns for order and symmetry, hygiene and cleanliness complains that the person who ate the last of the cookies should've placed the disposable plates in the trash can, but there's no point in wasting the brain power. The men I work with generally aren't flush with kitchen tidiness.

One other night like this—grim, dark, long—a night when I thought I'd die from hunger, I found a three-tier cake in a closed cardboard box to the left of the kitchen's door. The box was sitting on another table off to the side, easy to ignore. There was no labelling other than a small card that said, "Thank you" in flowing black ink, handwritten with care.

I looked inside because I knew I'd be working another five or six hours with nothing to eat; my stomach was beyond desperate. That night I was rewarded. Inside was a large, three-tier white cake covered in thin white icing and shredded coconut. Part of the top tier had already been eaten (I was too hungry to care). Next to the box was a stack of small Styrofoam bowls and, miracle of miracles, a large cup holding clean spoons. I served myself a double portion of this gorgeous cake—still fresh, with light vanilla flavoring, sweetened crunchy coconut.

Never mind that the cake my mother baked every year of my life for my birthday was a white cake with homemade white icing topped with sweetened, shredded coconut. Never mind that this was my favorite cake in the world—and had been since around age six. Never mind, that I'd already put in hours working in the rainy cold and would be on-duty for many more. I felt like I'd opened the doorway to heaven, and walking through it was sweet in every way possible.

I ate standing up, in case I got dispatched to a call or in case a supervisor came in and bitched about me taking too long at the station. I inhaled that chunk of exquisite cake, and I considered serving myself another double portion.

But I got dispatched to a call, and I knew I wouldn't be able to find a place in the patrol car to rest a teetering bowl of cake with a plastic spoon. Every night since then, when I walk into this cluttered room I await the appearance of another ethereal cake. My stomach muscles tense slightly in anticipation every time I enter this kitchen in the middle of a shift that's been too busy for eating, too remote from vending machines with their expensive treats, too fast for restroom breaks with calls dropping nonstop.

But, tonight is different. There is not one ounce of cake, cookies, sandwich, or any other assorted edible within sight—except for the small paper packets of salt and pepper. Not even stale Saltines. There is only empty, empty disappointment. Not enough to make me cuss when I find nothing to eat, but also not enough to keep me from looking in the middle of the night the next time I find myself starving. Starving, rushed, broke—it's predictable.

Of course, I haven't opened the refrigerators, but I wouldn't eat anything in there because all those containers belong to other officers. I remember the first time someone stole my lunch—clearly labeled "Cortez" with the date—at another police agency. All morning I'd been thinking about the homemade lasagna I'd brought. A red sauce redolent with garlic and fresh basil. The lingering complexity of real parmesan. I wanted to eat something that wasn't bureaucratic, that wasn't ugly, utilitarian, dirty, and low-bid. I wanted to taste my other life, my home—for a few precious minutes. When I went to the miniscule kitchen to nuke it, the distinctive container I'd brought from home sat empty in the trash can, still oozing tomato sauce. I couldn't believe it. If I'd been a few minutes earlier, I would have caught the jerk. After that, I got smarter. No more lunches requiring refrigeration. Only PBJ—a sandwich I could keep indefinitely inside a patrol car, in summer and in winter months. I added to my FTO store of advice: *don't put meat in your sandwiches if you keep them in the patrol car,* after one rookie got mild food poisoning from keeping his bologna sandwich in the patrol car for a half day in August. The harder lesson was: don't trust. Don't trust anyone, not even the sergeants and dispatchers—the only potential suspects inside the station when my lunch was stolen. Oh, yes, the civilian who ran Communications could've eaten my lasagna, but his office was far away from the kitchen and he said he was a vegetarian. A crazy world—these people who might save my life out on patrol, but who also might steal my only food during an eight-hour shift in a department too structured to allow an officer to go to any of the area restaurants, especially if that same officer had put herself out-of-service for lunch at the station.

As I walk down the sidewalk on the side of the station to my patrol car, I tell myself that I'm not hungry. The cold seeps into my trousers, past the insulating long johns and undershirt. My ears feel like they will fall off. Although, being in the station for a few minutes has helped my freezing toes and allowed my nose to warm. I focus on the job at hand. Later, when I go O/D, and drive home, will be the time for warmth, for hot food, for people who want to talk to me rather than at me. At home, it'll be good to pull off the heavy gun belt, to climb into bulky, warm clothes for the remainder of this wintry night. I'll put my electric blanket on high and it'll stay there the entire time I sleep. Some of the guys say they take long, hot showers first thing at home—just to warm up again. Their wives scream and push them away if they show up ice-cold under the sheets. I smile at the thought of my big-shouldered fellow patrol officers standing under hot water until they are rosy with warmth—just to please their wives. It takes a long time to warm up, even at home. A long time to sluice off the grit and loneliness of the streets we patrol. Sometimes, it takes a long time to figure out exactly what you want to eat.

Acquainted with Death

The busy maggots. Bloated body cavities and thickened necks. This dirty version of Death is an unfortunate reality for cops. Sometimes shit and piss, or blood leaking, spraying across our faces then up our noses when we inhale, dripping down our shirts, trousers, and ornate silver badges. Sometimes bone fragments, severed fingers, feet, ears, or entire heads. We don't get the Mr. Clean version.

Granted, not every shift, not every call-for-service. But Death's presence is always waiting, always lurking behind the door or dented dumpster, inside the cheap-walled mobile home or just behind the tree line's black lace. Death is always looking to jump out and grab someone. Any excuse will work—jealously, anger, love, hatred. Perhaps, inattention, incompetency, immaturity, mechanical failure, or just the luck of the draw. Ball point pens, hatchets, nylon cord, feather pillows that spew curlicued chicken feathers that make the crime scene techs sneeze. Maybe, the hardware used is a hammer, ice pick, scissors, or a two-by-four. Baseball bat, socket wrench, tennis racket, brick. Any favorable junction of motive and weapon. Any entry wound. Any kind of weather. Any time of day or night. In lavender dusk or in the pink promise of sunrise. In sunshine or wispy fog. Death is always waiting to ferry someone into final, darkest night.

Working your first "stinker"—cop jargon for a several-day-old rotting corpse—is its own peculiar rite of passage. Impossible to forget. Gruesome but telling, in ways that are important. Initially, you may cry, gag, puke, or refuse to go in. All that doesn't matter. The other officers want to know if you can think clearly when overpowered by noxious stimuli. All that counts is how you handle the smell and the sights when you do go in. One day the lives of the other officers on this scene may depend on your ability to react logically and tactically, to make split-second decisions in situations much worse than this. Are you level-headed? That's what they need to know. Can you still talk on the hand-held? Can you memorize a potential crime scene? Are you tactically aware? Remember that the killer may still be there, hidden in the closet or under the sink. The killer may even be the person who reported the DOA.

This officer I knew—a stocky Hispanic kid named Hernandez—told me the story of working his first stinker as a rookie on a humid July night choking with clouds of mosquitos. June bugs zooming towards the sodium-vapors lighting the cement, then dive-bombing anything white—like faces, or the small triangle of pure white T-shirt visible at their shirt fronts. The smell of death so strong, down in the apartment complex's parking lot, that every officer on the scene already knew the outcome to the call dispatched as "status check—elderly neighbor not seen for three days."

Of course, they picked Hernandez to make entry through the high, narrow window that had to be utilized because departmental policy wouldn't let them bust in the front door. So, in crawled the poor guy completely unable to see the interior of the room because his Streamlight rolled from his fingers and dropped inside when he hoisted his body over the ledge. He teetered on the edge, then slipped and fell inside, landing on top of the dead guy who was now a pillowy cushion of rotting flesh in a pool of slimy body fluids. I remember the officer telling me the story shaking his head in abbreviated side-to-side movements. *Yeah—that was bad. I fell right on top of him and all those maggots in the dark. The floor was so slippery that every time I tried to stand up I just fell back down on top of him.*

Eventually he located his flashlight, brushed off the vermin, found a light switch, opened the front door to let the other officers into the apartment. Later he was released from duty for a couple of hours to go home, shower, and change uniform. My guess is that he didn't try to wash the navy-blue trousers and shirt, or even his T-shirt, socks, and briefs. That he removed the brass from the shirt, cut off the patches, then trashed everything in someone else's blue metal dumpster as soon as he could. Some smells you can't get out—not from clothes, not from memory.

I didn't ask if he discarded the Streamlight. I would've wanted to toss it, but wouldn't have been able to afford a new one. So, I would've laid out thick layers of newsprint on the front porch, removed the batteries, wiped them off with paper towels, blotted the contacts, then rubbed them with a pencil eraser. Sprayed the exterior with Lysol and kept the flashlight. But I would've thought about where it'd been every time I wrapped my slender fingers around its sleek, cool metal shaft. Every time.

At the beginning of my career, I heard a lot of cop-to-cop advice for working DOAs. Typically, over breakfast at some fast-food joint since any of us could swallow the last three bits of scrambled egg on the way out the door if we were dispatched to a call while eating. And we often did inhale food as we scooted out the smudged glass doors with one ear cocked to the hand-held radio to memorize details of a dispatched call.

The advice always started out the same way: "Don't touch the body. Call the Sgt., then the ME.

"Don't ever, repeat ever, broadcast 'DOA' on the air—even if you can see a head rolling down the highway in one direction and a headless body cartwheeling in the opposite direction from the impact. Is Mr. John Q Citizen dead? Hell yes, he's dead. But on the airwaves, he's only a 'possible DOA.' And don't forget it. The supervisors will be pissed. The media will descend like vultures.

"If there are pills, you're screwed. The report will take you forever to write. Count all the pills in each bottle and the name of the medication. Name of the prescribing doc. Pharmacy, date dispensed, number of refills left—put it all in your report. Sometimes family members or caretakers steal certain kinds of pills. Sometimes Mr. DOA was helped along into Death's waiting arms by double or triple doses of certain pills. Could be a homicide.

"Put Vicks in your nostrils—for the smell. You know, the old-timers used to light cigars on the Homicide calls. Even the detectives who didn't smoke cigarettes would light up. Look at the older black-and-white photographs of detectives on murder scenes. Every single one of them is puffing a big, fat cigar as if his life depended on it. Nowadays, police officers use lemon air freshener inside dust masks. But no matter what you use, some of the real smell sneaks in.

"Memorize everything. Don't touch a thing.

"Treat every suicide as a homicide.

"Maggots bite hard. Stay out of their way."

There are some DOAs that no amount of advice can help an officer work. I think about the big-city veteran arson investigator whose every call for almost twenty years involved a burned-up corpse or a burned-up car. Sometimes, both. He told me that he could still see the face of a lovely, white female teen who died of smoke inhalation because the facility holding her had given her the wrong advice about what to do in the case of fire. They told her she could break the window's plate glass with a chair. But the glass didn't break—couldn't break—because it was plexiglass. Her mascara and eyeliner, still intact. Her ethereal face, serene—as if she didn't mind dying. Small hands with pink painted nails crossed over her chest. "I'm still angry about it, he said. It's been fifteen years, and I'm still pissed. She followed their advice and tried to break the window with a chair. Multiple times, but she couldn't."

I think about the call-for-service worked by ten patrol officers and supervisors. The call dropped as "unconscious infant male. Not breathing." Todd, a good friend of mine and life-long cop, was primary and first-in. Directed by the family to a back bedroom, he found a father CPRing the little boy like crazy. A pale, chubby little boy, aged four, but who looked two, max. A large towel was under the boy's neck with lots of bright red blood. The kid was already blue-green. Obviously, dead. But the dad continued CPR until EMS arrived and started working on him. Even though they also knew he was dead. At some point, they switched to organ-preservation mode—which my friend had never seen before or in the ten years since. The EMS guys took out two light blue plastic cases that could have come from any big-box home improvement store. They snapped open the lids. From one emerged drill bits, from the other a drill. They assembled the drill, exposed the little boy's shin, and drilled a ¾ inch hole in the leg. My friend—the father of three young children at the time and a military vet himself—tells me, "It was one of the most ghastly things I've ever seen."

Later he found out that the procedure was necessary to keep the organs intact—they needed that particular kind of hole, in that particular place, to insert a trocar to pump in the right kind of fluids fast, real fast. Todd pauses, then doesn't speak for a long time. I see the muscles in his tanned neck working to control his voice. "We wanted to let the parents go to the hospital. The little boy had been life-flighted. But we had to keep them there for a supervisor to interrogate them. To make sure it had really been an accident. It seemed to go on forever. Four or five days later a bunch of us were eating together. I don't know how we got on the subject of that little boy's death. One of the guys said, 'I'm not sleeping because I keep having nightmares.' Another guy says, 'This is the first good meal I've had since that call because I have no appetite. None at all.' I said how I wake up every thirty minutes or so with an urgent need to walk into my kids' rooms. To make sure they're okay. Still breathing." And so, the conversation went around the rectangular table of poker-faced men in blue uniforms. Fajitas cooling into cold strips of meat, bitten-off flour tortillas curling their edges into white skin on the heavy china plates. The ice melting in quart-sized iced-tea glasses because no one could move. "Yeah, we'd been playing the tough-guy game. You know, looking like you can take anything and everything. But inside, you feel it all."

I ask Todd how he feels about it now. He tells me that he can still see, plain as day, all the furniture in that apartment. He can still see the exact colors of everything and the pattern of the fabric on the couch in the first room he entered. Still see the chubby little boy's limp feet with no socks, thin gray shorts, a skimpy, white baseball-team T-shirt. Brown hair.

My friend saw that family a few days later for case follow-up. He says he was "insistent" about advising them to get some professional counseling for the one family member most involved in the accident causing the death. But who knows if they did or not? "It's the nature of our beast, Todd says. We cops don't have closure. We never see the people again.

"I know that family had to go home from the hospital

to the blood stain in the carpet where their little boy died in the back bedroom. My friend's voice grows stronger, but only briefly. It took me three years to put the demons to rest. I couldn't talk about it—it hurt to even talk about it."

The hardest DOA I worked was a totally different type of call-for-service. It was an elderly W/F who died in her upstairs bedroom in a middle-class neighborhood. A gray bedroom with a double bed, white sheets, and a pale-yellow bedspread. I was lucky—she wasn't a stinker or a child-death. But my own mother had died recently and, what's worse, unexpectedly. It was my first week back at work after her funeral. Both tragedies came in the middle of Houston's broiling dog days when the black tar inside asphalt streets melts and bubbles up during the day, and the relentless nights are filled with an extra helping of assaults, sexual assaults, agg robberies, and just plain 'ole greasy human meanness. No relief anywhere. Not from the grueling heat, not from the iron splinter of sadness and loss inside my chest.

I had a good corporal—he drove to my scene after the call dropped and said he'd work it himself if I was too upset to stay. When he asked, his blue eyes were lit with kind concern. He asked me more than once, and his eyes stayed on my face a long time. I thought I'd be okay, so instead of leaving, I remained, and he drove off after making a few notifications by phone. The only place to sit and maintain a visual of who came up the stairs was on the toilet lid in the old-fashioned, pink-and-pinker tiled bathroom down the hall from the simple bedroom with the corpse. You see, I had to make sure no one made entry into the bedroom except the ME and then the body-bag guys.

Like every cop on-duty, I had one ear trained to the handheld with its careful enunciation of dispatched calls and the gruff response of the officers. At one point, I heard the door to the woman's bedroom squeak open. Since I'd been sitting in that claustrophobic bathroom at the top of the stairs for hours, I was damn sure no one had walked into her bedroom. For a moment or two, I thought that woman had come back alive. And isn't it a crazy thing how hope rises in the human heart when complete loss is the only reality inside that same heart? When I heard that door creak open, for just a few seconds before I looked down the long unadorned hallway to see exactly who was walking out of that room, I hoped that it was my own mother come back to life. I hoped that God in His infinite mercy had released my momma to come back to me, her only daughter, her "pride and joy"—as she always said.

So, I paused. I thought about the ever-living soul. I even thought, for a milli-second, about hauntings and ghosts and Edgar Allen Poe's lurid tales and tortured inhabitants of those same stories. All this raced through my mind as the prolonged creaking of the door hinges reverberated along the skin of my arms.

Finally, I had to act. Swallowing whatever had risen in my throat and in my heart, I stepped around the corner to view the hallway. The DOA's cat—a huge, fluffy Persian—strolled down the hallway from the bedroom as if posing for a fashion spread in Milano. I guess the cat had missed her owner and gone searching for her, then walked back out pushing the door open wider. Or maybe the cat had been in the room all along and was exiting for the first time after the death. Who knows? Just to be sure the lady was still in the bed, I forced myself to walk the length of the carpeted hallway, open the bedroom door fully, and look inside. The DOA was in the same place, the same position: on her back, fully dressed, one knee cocked up, one leg straightened in front of her. Iron-gray hair that curled carefully below fleshy earlobes—just like my mom. Just like my own mom.

Eventually, the body-bag guys arrived. They came for

this poor lady with a gurney and acres of black plastic bisected by a rubberized industrial zipper. I watched as they tried to unfold her one bent leg, so they could strap her in horizontally to the gurney. We were all silent. After all, what's there to say in front of the dead?

Getting the loaded gurney down the narrow stairway with its devious turning angles was precarious. To me it looked like a tortured ballet—these beefy guys in black suit jackets straining to contain their muscles as they contorted their gurney with its heavy cargo. The stainless gurney's spring-loaded legs were too long, then not long enough, then too much, then in the way, and, finally, of assistance. At one point, I really thought they would be forced to drop the entire thing down the stairwell. It was too heavy, the angled stairs were fighting them—along with gravity and geometry, and every other damn physical law I could think of—velocity, circumference, diameter, decomposition. But, fortunately, the whole contraption didn't fall out of their large, capable, moon-white hands.

The excruciating reality was that she was someone else's mom—that thought never left me—I'd seen the photographs of a daughter downstairs. Plus, in so many ways, this DOA could be my mom—comfortably overweight, in a modest white blouse and double-knit, elastic-waisted pants. This house with its immaculate bathroom, the religiously vacuumed carpets. The sentimental, but meticulously dusted china ladies in billowing blue skirts on coffee tables. This could be my mom's house—almost.

Later, the corporal bumped me on the radio to meet him—he wanted to make sure I was still okay. Of course, I lied. *Sure, sure, I'm just fine.*

He was a decent supervisor who watched the faces of his troops carefully when he spoke to us, so he probably saw right through my pathetic, harmless little deceit. But he didn't point it out, and I'm glad he didn't. He handed over a few details I needed for my report, like the times of notifications. Then, he told me the origin of the call. The DOA's adult daughter had telephoned Dispatch from some other state. The two of them had been talking by telephone the night before about 2100 hours. The phone had gone dead in the middle of the conversation from her mother's end.

The corporal just shook his head—the daughter had waited almost fifteen hours to call us to check on her mom. I was too stunned to even react. The iron splinter that had entered my heart when I lost my own mother torqued just a little bit into a deeper pain. Like I said earlier, sometimes the greasy oil of human meanness, or failure to care, or stupidity just flows out and covers everything.

And maybe, just maybe, this is the hardest lesson of all—I can't stop other peoples' mistakes. As a police officer, I am involved in other peoples' tragedies, as well as their stupidities, their meanness, and their inattentions. My job is to stay level-headed and keep my heart out of whatever is going on. Sometimes, the only way to keep calm is to let other peoples' emotions wash off as if you were adamantine steel. Sometimes, the only way to keep calm is to absorb and absorb and absorb until you can go home, maybe pray, maybe talk to someone you trust. But if you absorb feelings, you also must maintain control over your own center of logic so that your decision-making on the scene isn't flawed. Sometimes, sleep is the only remedy—the only blackness that is safe—if there are no nightmares. Or, as my career cop-buddy Kenny used to say, "I get home. Some nights, I drink 'til the bottle's empty. Those are the nights when it's been real bad."

Sometimes people say that part of what they hate about cops is that we're like robots—too calm, too self-controlled, too logical. We bear this criticism, like everything else, in silence. You see, inside the cool silence resides each officer's anchors: the irrational belief in goodness, strength, and justice; the deep trust in just a few fellow human beings, and, for many, the spiritual connection to Almighty God. Inside this same stillness rests a belief in the essential role of police officers in a lawful society. If we didn't possess these touchstones, we would have no indemnity against the crazy horrors of human behavior. Otherwise we would be incinerated by the raging conflagrations of other peoples' erratic behaviors and devastating cruelty; otherwise, we too would go up in flame until nothing was left but cold, dry ash. Bitter to the taste and poisonous.

Supervisors

I stare at my dead sergeant. He lies inside the folded white satin of this, his last resting place. He is wearing our agency's uniform, everything improbable at this stiff horizontal, rather than at the commonplace vertical of a living, breathing man. All his brass is shiny, too shiny, as if polished for the funeral home's overhead spotlights earned for him by cancer too early, as it has been for so many men I've policed with. I've seen the tall and the strong transformed into shrunken old men with drawn lips, years before their time.

He was a good sergeant, one of the best I've encountered in years of police work. In a pre-cell-phone era, he was the one who showed each new officer in his unit a little tan book of telephone numbers. He'd page through it with a stubby, freckled thumb and say, "You need something on a scene, you call me. Any time day or night. I've got contacts in every agency in Texas. I'll find you an answer. But call me *first*. Before the on-duty supervisor, before the lieutenant. You call me before you do anything."

Because he respected us and the job we were trying to do, and because we trusted him, we would call him from a scene. The three A.M. traffic stop gone south, or the domestic-turned-cluster. "Hey, Sarge, I'm sorry to wake you up, but . . ." He knew how hard it could be to find a magistrate in the middle of the night; he knew how to get a DRE (Drug Recognition Expert) at a scene from another agency across town, or the right kind of K-9 unit. He took care of us by helping us do our jobs, and we did our dead-level best to do whatever he asked. He didn't have to give orders. We respected him enough that we wanted to do good work for him. And we always did, or tried to.

All of us at the station realized how much he cared for teens. He'd been on the streets long enough to predict the tailspin into failed lives so many would take once they found the wrong set of friends. One shift I had a reported runaway, female. She was maybe fifteen, or sixteen. While I was taking the report from a distraught mom, Sarge checked by. He knew the family and had some ideas about where the daughter was hiding out. Luckily, he was right.

Later, when the silent but defiant girl was back at home, I saw Sarge do his best to talk some sense into her. She sat in an armchair in the den holding a navy velour blanket as if it was a shield. The mother stood at the kitchen counter red-faced and sniffling as she wavered from anger to relief, and back again. Sarge brought over the yellow pages to the girl and handed it to her. She was doing the teenage, passive-aggressive-can't-be-bothered rendition of bitch. He told her to look up "Funerals." She used her tongue to slide a wad of gum back toward her molars and yawned. He told her again. She nonchalantly thumbed through the flimsy pages until she found it. He squashed the page under an emphatic index finger. "Choose which one of those you want," he said. She raised her big brown eyes up to his face.

He didn't waver, but punched down the page again. "You choose which funeral home you want for your burial, girl, because before this time next year you'll be dead." He then turned to her mom and motioned her over. "Bring over a pad of paper and a pen. Your daughter is going to tell you where her funeral will be at." The mom walked over to the chair. The girl sat holding the book, for the first time tonight looking like she might cry. He turned and looked at her, "You better get rid of those new friends of yours because if you stick with them, you'll be dead in a year. Twelve months—count 'em out. That's all you got. I've seen it plenty of times. You got too much going for you to want to die. You know how many don't have a mom to love them? You think about it hard and talk to your mom. I want to hear from her later that you two had a good talk."

Sarge was one of the Vietnam-era supervisors. The guys who had fought in Vietnam understood that a sergeant's function was to keep his troops from being butchered. Translated into LE, the Vietnam-era police sergeants looked after their officers, getting them proper training, essential info, and steering them clear of whatever might go up to the lieutenant or captain as a complaint.

The post-Vietnam-era sergeant wanted to be the one butchering his troops and created an adversarial relationship with the men he supervised. This meant he didn't trust his troops and often used a steady verbal style of ridicule, insults, and deliberate put-downs. This type of sergeant always assumed his men were in the wrong and must be spied upon or tricked to ensure correct behavior. Sometimes this attitude resulted in a supervisor dogging out a competent officer until that officer became so nervous that his decision-making went to hell, thus creating the documented instances that would form a reason to fire him. Supervision became an extended cat-and-mouse game with deceptions rampant. No one except the supervisor ever won, and the inevitable payoff among the remaining troops was paranoia, frustration, and cagey hatreds.

I had learned from a long-time female cop up North to be careful of this type of post-Vietnam supervisor when I was still in the police academy. "Your most dangerous enemies are always back at the station," she'd informed me. "The criminals on the streets—they're the most obvious danger, true enough. But your fellow officers and supervisors who lie about you back at the station—that's the biggest danger to your career." I hated the fact that this might be true, but when I glimpsed and experienced a few of these difficult supervisors, I saw the validity of her wisdom.

My first sergeant was a female, and her style of supervision was the post-Vietnam-era type. Before working for her, I was primed to like her. After all, she was rumored to have had a long career with a big police agency—which I respected—and we both were minorities of a different stripe. How could she not like a rookie like me—smart, eager to learn, in excellent physical shape, single with no kids to cause multiple call-offs. My assumption was laughable, in retrospect. It would be months before I could see that the salient features of everything I had struggled years to attain—an educated brain, the ability to speak in public, a svelte muscularity—she read as an insult. I turned her stomach—that much she made clear, even in the simplest of shift tasks, like assigning lunch breaks during roll call. And there I was—stuck on her shift for over a year. Even some of the more experienced male officers on my shift—I found out later—went to her "off-record" to tell her she was being too unfair to me. "Level-off," they told her. "Cortez is a good officer." It didn't work.

Even my best friend Angela, hired on the same day as I, couldn't figure out why that supervisor always treated me so differently than she treated the other officers. I stubbornly refused to believe—and still refuse to believe—it had anything to do with ethnicity or race. Certainly, not on my end. How could it? Angela, my sweet friend and fellow officer, was black and we were close in a way that only going through FTO phases together makes happen. We spent half of our off-duty time on the phone with each other and did everything together—alterations for uniforms, working out, buying lace bras to wear for our respective lovers, researching courses at the community college. Most importantly, Angela always had my back, as I did for her, in the swirling gossip and fluctuating friendships of that small, unhappy department.

While I worked under this first sergeant, I saw a police management textbook in a library. In its chapter entitled "Supervision," it listed the qualities necessary for a supervisor: integrity, honesty, fairness. My already-acquired street cop's cynicism didn't keep me from wishing it was true, even though we all heard the rumors that one of the married lieutenants was having an affair with a Record's clerk, drinking alcohol on-duty, and trying to seduce any civilian employee impressionable enough to be cowed by the inch-long brass bars on each of his sloping shoulders. I hadn't met Sarge yet, or a supervisor like him, so I could only dream of a supervisor who cared deeply about and respected his officers, who didn't use sarcastic remarks about one officer in front of other officers, who understood that if we were trusted rather than mistrusted, we were capable and eager to excel at our jobs.

Admittedly, it was a hard-pressed department. Small, used mainly as a stepping stone to jobs with bigger agencies, it had a galloping turnover rate that made morale a laughable term, doubtlessly for the supervisors, as well as for the troops. Yet, couldn't the department have found a way to harness the drive to fight crime in those of us who wanted to do so? More specialized training? A drug-sniffing dog? A DWI task force? Bike Patrol? The answer was always: "No." We assumed it was because the Chief didn't want higher arrest stats, since more training always translates into more arrests. So, we made our petty assumptions after each refusal, and wilted a little more under the smart epaulets and shiny badges. Had we given up better paying jobs, marriages, weekends off, seeing friends and family on birthdays, Sundays, weddings and funerals to baby-sit rather than arrest? And the supervisors who baby-sat us? Surely, they saw how each of us became predictably depressed and surly. Our hardened faces at roll call reflecting to the sergeants the cold realities of boredom and passivity. We were kindling ready for the full-blown flame of active crime-fighting. Instead, we barely kept alive its small, rusted flame deep down in the embers of our hearts.

Luckily, the few decent supervisors—not normally on my shifts—made it worth our while to work there. They set stellar examples by never complaining, sneaking in a little pragmatic training when they could, being even-keeled with their moods and emotions. The good ones were our heroes; the incompetent ones, a job condition we couldn't change and tried to survive.

Looking at my dead sergeant, I recall the good he did on the job: all the meetings on his off-duty hours with citizens to find out where they perceived crimes were occurring—the illegal drugs being purchased or used, the stop signs being run, the school-zone speed limits not being respected. After those meetings with neighborhoods, he'd come to us at the beginning of a shift and pass out specialized assignments based on what he'd heard and the stats he'd run. This created a way for us to be proactive in helping the community amid the largely reactive job of answering calls-for-service. These special tasks with unique responsibilities gave us a way to be creative in our police work and established a clear tie to feeling that we were indeed helping the neighborhoods in a way they would appreciate.

Sarge had amassed enough bureaucratic expertise to generally figure out how to maneuver within the command structure to get clearance on training, equipment, or projects that would help us fight crime. Sometimes he could even gain a commitment from another police agency who had undercover capabilities or other specialized equipment to help address a situation in our patrol area. He had mastered the art of tactful strength in talking to the higher-ups; he had learned how to motivate us to produce results that could be proven by typical crime-fighting stats: the number of arrests, cases cleared, written "atta' boys" from the citizens. Two different types of results at two different ends of the totem pole, two differing types of conversations, two differing sets of stress, but one goal: elevate the safety of the people in the community.

Sarge was committed to teaching his officers. After all, he'd been in policing over thirty years. He began in the minimal-training era when a new police officer, particularly in rural communities, on his first day was thrown the keys to the patrol car, and maybe to the jail, and told, "Get out there on patrol." Other police friends have spoken of being nineteen or twenty years of age, bean-pole skinny, in a police uniform on day one with no police academy, and the only officer on duty. One friend still shakes his head and laughs as he says, "I was so skinny that I couldn't have held my own in a fight with the town drunk, or his wife. Luckily, he was still sleeping it off. Otherwise, he would have wiped up the barroom floor with me and I would've looked like a porcupine from the wood splinters." Sarge had also lived through the virulent hatreds and radical violence against police in the Hippie Era of the 1960s. He was a smart, thoughtful man who could put a larger framework of understanding around any situation or any craziness within or outside the department.

He'd pause, look off in the distance, then his eyes would come back to look directly at you. He'd say, with a slight smile on his freckled face, "You know, Cortez, there's no way to predict people. If someone does something crazy on a traffic stop, you didn't cause it. Run a tape, then call me. Then call the on-duty supervisor. Be prepared for craziness. Make sure you don't get hurt. Okay?" The moment's pause at the end made you know he cared because he always waited to make sure you responded to his "Okay?" and he kept looking into your eyes to see if you meant it.

Never raising his voice, never assuming we had screwed-up, never blaming us for circumstances beyond our control, and always, always telling the truth—that was how Sarge operated. And if he determined that any of his officers had made a mistake, he educated the officer how to do it differently next time. He sat down alone with that officer at the small, round, plastic table in a repurposed office, closed the beige drapes, and went through, step-by-step, how to do it better; he also illustrated the rationale behind the decisions. He cared that each officer understood what he said, and this combination of care and explanation worked magic: you never forgot how to analyze and handle that particular situation.

His training was particularly effective because policing is a judgment-call "business." Each situation must be assessed, then handled, and it might be handled in a hundred different ways—all of which are legal. Yet each officer's manner of logical thinking and decision-making must fall within the law, within departmental policy, and within the department's current style of policing—that's why the careful teaching of the decision-making process is so important. Sarge knew this and took the time to do it—without ridicule, without ire, without blame. Even without cussing.

I didn't know Sarge personally, so I don't know if he had moments of darkness and hopelessness about LE at night at home with his wife. But he didn't have those moments on-duty and that was what I, and the other troops who he supervised, needed. So, in this respect, he was a true leader—not someone we went out beer-drinking with or partied with, but someone who held himself above us—just a little—because of his vast experience on the job and his willingness to fight the battles we couldn't fight for ourselves with the higher-ups or the community.

Each of us in his unit stand a few moments in silent tribute and salute him before we leave the coffin's side. It is here, at this exact moment, that tears come to my eyes. The salute is emblematic for the respect he earned and the respect he showed each of us in turn. Even in an era of exaggeration, each of us knows that Sarge is irreplaceable.

Here Are My Lists

My goals: don't get killed, don't get injured, don't be stupid—in order of priority. Sounds simple, doesn't it? But like anything else that sounds easy in police work, it isn't.

Here are a few rules—aphorisms by and for police based on real-life experience.

See what you think.

Short List: How to Avoid Getting Killed

1. There's a difference between cover and concealment. The first stops bullets; the second doesn't. You best know the difference.

    First corollary: your car door won't stop a bullet.
    Second corollary: a mailbox won't stop a bullet.
    Third corollary: another person's body doesn't always stop a bullet.
    Fourth corollary: concrete block walls don't always stop bullets. Bricks don't either.

    Conclusion: Good luck if someone is shooting at you.

2. The wife may have called you for help, but that doesn't mean she wants hubby to go to jail. She'll turn on you.

3. Never park directly in front of a convenience store. Park to the side, but before you do anything, find the clerk through the window and make sure he's doing something normal.
4. There's a One-Plus rule. If you take one gun off a suspect, look for the second one. Same holds true for two guns, or three. Knives, same way.
5. Wear your vest every time you're in uniform. No exceptions. End of story.
6. If you light up your spotlight on a suspect, don't be sitting in the driver's seat. If he shoots, that's where he'll aim.
7. No car is ever stopped by standing in an intersection and holding up your hand. When you direct traffic, don't stand in front of the cars. Stand to the side.
8. Nine-year-olds kill cops and so do ninety-year-olds. Males and females. Don't trust anyone.
9. Be polite. Be professional. But always have a plan how to kill everyone in the room.

Short List: Things You Can't Avoid When You Get Killed or Shot

1. If you get gut-shot, you better not have eaten. It'll be a real mess for the doc.
2. Don't get killed working undercover. The turd will say he didn't know you were the po-po, and the jury will feel sorry for him.
3. On a traffic stop, if someone wants to kill you, there's nothing you can do about it. Nothing. Unless he misses his first shot, then you cap his ass.
4. Don't wear underwear with holes. The ER nurses will laugh. (Though, if you're dead, it don't matter.)

5. Just because you're dead, you're not a saint. All the ones who hated you before will still hate you. Everyone who liked you before will still like you.
6. After a shooting incident, you'll lose your hearing for a few days. Maybe, it'll come back. Maybe not.
7. Everyone who wanted to sleep with your wife before you were dead, will.

Short List: Rules for Eating On-Duty

1. Don't accept food from anyone. Period.
2. Don't eat anywhere you can't see the food being prepared.
3. Never expect a "discount." If it's given as a gift, accept it graciously but always leave a hefty tip.
4. No catsup or barbeque sauce at the drive-thru. When you wreck, it looks like blood. If you drip down the front of your shirt, it looks like blood.
5. Eat the fries first, in case you get a call. They spill in the car and get cold quick. Sandwiches can be boxed up.
6. Don't expect to eat every shift. Carry some power bars in your patrol bag.
7. If you're going to break any rules regarding dinner/lunch breaks, invite the sergeant along. That way, it's a "supervisory meeting" and an exception to the rules.

Short List: Rules for Traffic Stops

1. Never ever, repeat ever, put your head or arm inside a violator's vehicle. You're just asking to be dragged.
2. Don't take your eyes off the violator or the passenger. The passenger can kill you just like the driver can.

3. Every car has at least seven equipment violations. As long as a violator cusses you out, you keep writing.
4. Don't place a DL between your teeth to hold it. You don't know where that dude's hands were last and, for sure, he pissed sometime today.

Short List: Generic Rules

1. The Feds are dicks to local PD.
2. The only fair fight is the one you're losing.
3. Know where the good, clean bathrooms are in your beat. Office buildings are the best.
4. The naked ones are always the ugliest ones. Dead or alive.
5. Never chase someone on foot beyond your limits. If you don't have the strength to fight once you put your hands on him, you'll die or get very-much-bad-hurt.
6. Be nice until it's no longer possible.
7. If she walks out in sexy underwear, have a planned exit. Keep the supervisor informed.
8. Badge-bunnies are more dangerous than 171s (crazies).
9. Do not point your patrol car toward to station to O/D one minute before the exact time it takes to get there—no matter how hot your date. If you try to squeeze in one extra minute, a call will drop.
10. Buy good footwear. Don't go cheap.
11. Don't "John Wayne" it. If you need back-up, call for it.
12. Keep your gun in its holster. Both your guns.
13. Don't be afraid to pat down a dude's crotch during an arrest. You find all kinds of illegal stuff squirreled away next to Pancho and Lefty.

14. Don't lean up against a wall in a house or apartment. The roaches will start running on you.
15. Would you rather be judged by twelve or carried by six?

And, most importantly:

1. Go home to your loved ones at the end of your shift.

After Many Years

I wish I could explain how my expectation of making the world a better place, as a police officer, was changed into careful coldness. Not an uncaring coldness, but rather, a distant coldness that became comfortable, that became who I am, that became the most salient and valuable component of my emotional armor in surviving the mental havoc of working the streets. I'd like to be able to explain how my optimism became guarded cynicism, and how what I thought was the real possibility of brighter results flickered and became cold ash.

I don't regret that this change happened because it is a prudential response reflective of my LE reality, and thus, serves to protect me: heart, mind, and body. *It's the streets* is what veteran cops say as rookies go through this predictable, hard-knock transition. It becomes evident in officers' posture, in their eyes. It's the hardness and certainty that I admired in my friend Sgt. Chuck all those years ago before I became a police officer myself. It's more than the permanent darkness of exhaustion in the fragile skin below the eyes; it's more than a torso's stiffness inside the restrictive ballistic vest. It's the learned response to potential violence and death.

Sometimes, it happens after the first time a police officer is beat up. As my good friend Gary, a life-long cop, says, "You can tell when the females [officers] have their asses whipped by some drunk. After that, no more make up. Hair, straight back in a ponytail. They don't care anymore what they look like—they've learned it don't make no difference. Whupped is whupped."

Sometimes the transition is ushered in by a civilian's deception during or after a scene worked by a police officer. The best FTO I had, who eventually became a well-respected police chief at another agency, told this story from his first policing job: "I made a traffic stop on the feeder of a freeway. A W/F. She cried, and I felt sorry for her, so I didn't write a ticket, not even a warning. Maybe, ten minutes max to run her vehicle and check her insurance. She drove off. What I didn't know was that she was driving home after meeting her boyfriend at a motel. When the husband sees how late she is, she says I held her and made all kinds of sexual overtures, kept her a couple of hours and forced her into sex with me to get out of the ticket. Big investigation. Took weeks. I got lucky because her lover was found out. Could've cost me my career—her lies. Always drop paper on a traffic stop. Warning or the real deal—it don't matter."

Stories like this one began the chill in my bones that would gradually take over my entire existence. I learned that to trust on the streets is to die or get injured. As a cadet in the police academy—as in every police academy—I watched tapes of police officers shot, stabbed, throttled. I memorized the statistics for the overwhelmingly high probability that if someone took my firearm from my holster or hand that he/she would kill me with it. I learned that to lose my gun to another person would be to sign my own death certificate.

Yet, it wasn't the fear of death that wore me down, or even the relentless necessity of trying to be tactically astute to lower the probability of injury or death. After all, tactics become second nature. What wore me down was the steady stream of failed lives in most suspects and criminals I encountered. Sometimes, complainants too. I became an expert in other peoples' tragedies, sadnesses, angers, losses, and sometimes just plain 'ole stupid decisions—as each police officer must do.

Through experience, I learned that good advice to people on a scene rarely does any good, long-term. I witnessed people—young and old—make the same illegal decisions again and again, no matter how uplifting and invigorating the speech from a police officer. I watched abused women and men, still purple with bruises, scabs not yet healed over, the black thread of stitches still laced through faces, noses and lips, return to homes with documented family violence and the abuser still in residence. I observed kids start hanging out with the wrong crowd and progress from bored to criminal in a few months—no matter how many times the kid or the parents were counseled. And lies—there's no end to the lies.

I reached several conclusions. First, that I must do my job as I agreed to do it when I took my oath of office. Among other things, this means I cannot forget my commitment to protect the innocent, the crime victims. Despite the embarrassed silence and continued vulnerability of some crime victims, their legal and psychic needs inform all our American society since laws are to protect them, while pointing toward what will substantiate the common good. These people, and sometimes animals too, that are crime victims, are owed justice. Those who choose to perform illegal actions—the criminals—cannot and should not control the tenor of everyday life in America. Thus, my job as a police officer is to do my best—just as every police officer must do—so that our society will be made better, short-term and long-term.

The next conclusion I reached is a direct result of both major and minor disappointments rife in law enforcement, as in any bureaucracy or industry. The job I do—if I do it well—is basically done for my own integrity as a person and as an employee. It is not done for external rewards or exterior commendation. It is I alone who must look at myself in a mirror each night and each morning and answer the fundamental question that each person should ask: did I live up to the highest standards of behavior I could today?

In another world, in other times, the asking of self about living up to "the best" one could be would have been called *holiness*. Now, in a culture burdened with secularism, we are afraid of this word. Instead, our society talks about "best practices," "values," "goals," and "efficiencies." Differing terminology does not obscure the goal: to do the best possible to the highest ethical standards within the stated constraints.

And the constraints on police budgets and police officers approach the legendary: limited funds, equipment in constant need of upgrading or replacement, weather, visibility, health risks through disease (e.g. TB, HIV/AIDS, hepatitis) and vermin (e.g. lice, fleas, roaches, silverfish, wasps, spiders, rats, maggots), risk of injury, burn-out, death. And always, there is the completely unpredictable, crazy happenings that occur when violent and hostile folks choose to act. To say nothing of the mundane: a policing career lost when an undercover officer goes up a staircase in a warrant raid and steps on a rotten board that gives way, injuring his knee permanently and forcing a premature end to his LE career.

This notion of doing the best possible job also underscores the necessity of foregrounding the fact that policing is a *job*. A poorly paid job, in general. A job that is misunderstood by an increasingly large number of people, regrettably. Writing citations, taking someone to jail for breaking the law—this is a job that I, and other police officers, agreed to do. Whether or not an individual police officer considers his job to also be a vocation—as I do—is beside the point. Once a police officer takes an oath of office he has a *duty to act* when the law is broken.

Talking and writing about all of this is hard because on the streets there is no room for the niceties and nuances of philosophy. A police officer must act and react. Every officer tries to make reasoned judgements according to the law and departmental Policy and Procedure. What I believe and act out of—the law—must be so deeply ingrained in my inner being that it becomes an ultimate from which my actions and attitudes originate, no matter the circumstances, no matter the cost. The law must be written on a heart and soul—on your very being. It is this integrity of purpose and action that makes for a good cop—a person who is clear about what he is fighting for and why. I believe it is this coherence of belief and action that can allow for a small participation in the age-old concept of warrior—the person who does the right thing, for the right reason. This is why veteran cops who've policed in the worst ghettos in America say, *police fight in the war that never ends—the war against the criminals.* But it's also said by the tall, thin, muscular guys who work in Computer Crimes and the faintly nerdy Feds who study balance sheets and bank transactions for illegal money. All police know this, and, for sure, the criminals—both domestic and international—know this.

One day, or perhaps one night, I may respond to a call-for-service that involves you or someone you love. Maybe one of my policing brothers or sisters will respond to your need. We will be there after a criminal burglarizes your elderly mother's house, sodomizes her, then tries to set her on fire. I will be there to conduct the sexual assault investigation after your thirteen-year-old daughter is convinced to skip school by an older boy she knows who gets her drunk on Tito's, then engages in various forms of sex that she doesn't quite remember later. I will be there when people involved in illegal dog fights leave over twenty dogs chained to stakes outside of individual dog houses to starve to death behind a tall boarded fence on a large parcel of land. I, or a fellow police officer, will be the one to walk by each chained skeleton and vow to put the right person in jail by conducting a well-documented, thorough investigation, then writing an excellent report and testifying in court.

In all these cases, and so many more, I or another police officer, will look at corpses, bodies, scenes of destruction, tapes of child porn, or explicit text messages that we would rather not view. I do it because I believe the job I do is important. Besides, it is the job I agreed to do. A job that requires rock-solid clarity of purpose supported by training and that distant coldness the streets have taught me. All of this enables me to do the best job I can do for you, for my employer, and for my own integrity before Almighty God.

There's a reason the badge is worn on the left side of the chest—on the side of the heart. We men and women can do *this* job, this job that no one else wants to do, because we care, because we are invested enough in each person in our society that we're willing to die to protect complete strangers—that's why we wear the badge, that's why it's worn over our hearts, that's why we're cops.

Glossary and Abbreviations

171—This is part of the code that is a historical remnant of the 10-Codes System formerly used by officers to communicate with the Dispatcher. 171 indicates a mentally deranged subject.

ADA—Assistant District Attorney

Agg—aggravated, which in layman's terms means that a weapon was used in the commission of a crime

CAD—Computer-Aided Dispatch System

CJ—Criminal Justice

DI—Drill Instructor

DRE—Drug Recognition Expert

Driving hot—Driving a patrol vehicle with lights and sirens on

DWI—Driving While Intoxicated. This abbreviation can be pronounced in two ways: 1) with each letter individually verbalized, or 2) DEE-WEE.

Gig line—Intersection at the hips of shirt flap, belt buckle, and zipper flap. This requires starting the belt into belt flaps on the left. If this is done correctly, then the beginning edge of the belt buckle will line up vertically with the other two flaps.

Juvie—Juvenile

LE—Law Enforcement

LT—These two letters are pronounced individually and are a standard verbal nickname for a lieutenant.

MDT—Mobile Data Terminal is a computerized device typically installed in a police car in the front seat between the driver's and passenger-side seats to allow access to law enforcement-related data needed for investigatory work while in the field.

ME—Medical Examiner

Military Time—A method of telling time that is based on a 24-hour period with each hour identified by its relationship to midnight which is zero hours. This system eliminates the need for A.M. and P.M. markers.

O/D—Off-duty

P&P—Policy and Procedure

Probationary—A new police officer who has not yet been released from his probation period.

Ropers—Historically, Roper-style boots are one type of Western riding boot. The Roper is distinguished by a lower flat and squared heel which is shaped to the boot top and less than one inch. Typically, it has a shorter shaft, ending between mid-thigh and ankle, than a standard cowboy boot, and has a rounded toe.

Shop—Police vehicle (car)

S/O—Sign-on for duty

TABC—Texas Alcohol and Beverage Commission

Unit—This may refer to a police vehicle or a police officer or to a specialized group within a police department.

W/F, B/F—Standardized abbreviations for white female, black female

CPSIA information can be obtained
at www.ICGtesting.com
Printed in the USA
LVOW03s2304220318
570873LV00001B/10/P

9 781680 031430